Business Process Automation with Salesforce Flows

Transform business processes with Salesforce Flows to deliver unmatched user experiences

Srini Munagavalasa

BIRMINGHAM—MUMBAI

Business Process Automation with Salesforce Flows

Group Product Manager: Alok Dhuri

Publishing Product Manager: Kushal Dave

Senior Content Development Editor: Rosal Colaco

Technical Editor: Vidhisha Patidar

Copy Editor: Safis Editing

Associate Project Manager: Deeksha Thakkar

Indexer: Rekha Nair

Production Designer: Prafulla Nikalje

DevRel Marketing Coordinators: Deepak Kumar and Mayank Singh

Business Development Executive: Puneet Kaur

First published: November 2023

Production reference: 1231123

Published by Packt Publishing Ltd.
Grosvenor House
11 St Paul's Square
Birmingham
B3 1RB, UK.

ISBN 978-1-83508-925-5

www.packtpub.com

Om Shri Ganeshaya Namah

I would like to thank my wife, Sunanda, and my children, Sravan and Sai, for all their support and encouragement; my Packt team, for their guidance and keeping me on track; and my reviewers, for providing valuable feedback. Finally, thanks to my family members, friends, and all my colleagues at work, who helped me learn and grow from my experiences

- Srini Munagavalasa

Contributors

About the author

Srini Munagavalasa has more than 20 years of global IT experience in Salesforce CRM and PRM, SAP CRM, and HR. He has a passion for learning about new and emerging technologies and products and prototyping and implementing solutions that result in customer satisfaction and business benefits. He has authored more than 10 articles on CRM, HR, and project management with **Wellesley Information Services** (**WIS**). He has also presented papers at Salesforce Dreamforce and SAP Sapphire/ASUG. He is currently working as a VP at Salesforce COE at MUFG Americas. He has a bachelor's degree in metallurgical engineering and holds a post-graduate diploma in operations management. He has worked with renowned companies such as CA Tech, IBM, The Walt Disney Company, and PwC.

About the reviewer

Lars Malmqvist is a 32x certified Salesforce CTA and has spent the past 15 years in the Salesforce ecosystem building advanced solutions on the platform. Currently, he works as a partner in the management consultancy, Implement Consulting Group, focusing on supporting large Nordic Salesforce clients in their transformation journeys. For the past five years, he has been focused on issues around using AI on Salesforce, combining this with academic research in deep learning and argumentation. He has published two books, *Architecting AI Solutions on Salesforce*, and *Salesforce Anti-Patterns*, both with Packt Publishing.

I would like to acknowledge my family, Damiana, Ada, and Pino. Without you, nothing else would make sense.

Table of Contents

7

Flows Using Apex Sharing   83

8

Optimizing and Troubleshooting Flows   95

Part 3: Flow Orchestration

9

Flow Orchestration   121

10

Compose and Orchestrate Business Processes   139

Assessments   153

Index   159

Other Books You May Enjoy   164

Preface

This book will begin by quickly exploring the various aspects of process automation using Salesforce Flow. We will cover the nuts and bolts of flow and execution order, along with distinct flow types and troubleshooting techniques to manage your processes.

The book will also explore flow orchestration tools that let us compose and orchestrate complex business processes. In *Part 3*, we will take a complex sales scenario, use the knowledge gained from *Parts 1* and *2*, and automate a complex business process. You will get an opportunity to follow the end-to-end business process flow, automate the business process via flow orchestration, and learn how to demystify and simplify business process automation.

By the end of this book, you will be confident in automating your business processes smoothly and without any hassle.

Who this book is for

This book is for system admins, technical team members, and business analysts with a good understanding of Salesforce CRM software who want to learn ways to effectively automate their business processes using Salesforce Flows.

What this book covers

Chapter 1, Process Flows – Understanding Business Requirements, explores and helps us understand the documented requirements and the process flows. Only after a good understanding of business requirements and process steps can we confidently move on to the next step to determine if a process step can be a potential candidate for automation.

Chapter 2, Identification of Functional Requirements for Automation, covers solution design aspects of functional requirements. We will explore in detail how to split requirements into tasks that can be automated. We will dive deep and discuss the rationale for every task we intend to automate.

Chapter 3, Business Process Features to Automate, discusses why it is important to allocate enough time and prioritize requirements automation. Prioritizing does not mean bringing requirements to the top as they come in from business users, but rather distributing around different releases on the road map to add optimum value to the overall business. You will be able to learn methods to identify important tasks and provide business value.

Chapter 4, Flow Building Blocks, Triggering, and Entry Conditions, covers the main building blocks of Salesforce Flows used in Flow Builder - elements, connectors, and resources. Then we will discuss ways to trigger the flow and entry/exit conditions. You will be able to understand the concepts of Salesforce Flows and get equipped to start creating flow at your organization.

Chapter 5, Salesforce Order of Execution, explores the **Order of Execution** (**OOE**) of how your system runs various tasks in the backend. OOE was critical in general for technical teams only in the past, but now it is more important for every salesforce team member. Understanding the OOE with real-world examples will help you get comfortable, and this chapter will explore the concepts of execution so as not to cause any technical debt.

Chapter 6, Types of Salesforce Flows, explores five basic types of flows to automate our business processes. You will gain a deep understanding of scenarios for each of the flow types - screen flows, record trigger flow, schedule-trigger flow, platform event-triggered flow, and autolaunched flows.

Chapter 7, Flows Using Apex Sharing, discusses a very important feature and share records via Flows that are not available by any means other than Apex coding. Now with flow, we have this feature available where you, as an admin, shall be able to perform these actions without code.

Chapter 8, Optimizing and Troubleshooting Flows, explores and helps us learn how to use the Flow Builder debug window to optimize and troubleshoot flows. Anything developed either declaratively or using code will run into some kind of bug, and you need a tool to be able to understand the error message and what it means. We will discuss a few scenarios to effectively debug and make sense of the flow for the users.

Chapter 9, Flow Orchestration, explores and sees how we can streamline and enable complex business processes using flow orchestration. We will explore and learn flow building blocks, and how these blocks work, and then discuss steps to create a flow orchestration. We will explore ways to monitor and streamline our orchestration as well as key considerations to make your orchestration effective.

Chapter 10, Compose and Orchestrate Business Processes, in this last chapter, we will look at a practical scenario, a simplified real-world business requirement, business process flow, and finally a flow orchestration that meets our business needs. We will look at making our orchestration efficient, effective, simple, and usable.

Assessments contains all the answers to the questions from all the chapters.

Conventions used

There are a number of text conventions used throughout this book.

`Code in text`: Indicates code words in text, database table names, folder names, filenames, file extensions, pathnames, dummy URLs, user input, and Twitter handles. Here is an example: " The `HAVING` clause is used to filter rows resulting from the `GROUP BY` clause."

A block of code is set as follows:

```
SELECT <select list>
     FROM <object source>
     WHERE <search condition>
     GROUP BY <group by expression>
     HAVING <search condition>
     ORDER BY <order expression>
```

Bold: Indicates a new term, an important word, or words that you see onscreen. For instance, words in menus or dialog boxes appear in **bold**. Here is an example: "Since we want this to be launched at the discretion of the Account Manager, in this scenario, we created a custom link called **Customer Upgrade** on the **Account** page under the **Details** section."

> Tips or important notes
> Appear like this.

Get in touch

Feedback from our readers is always welcome.

General feedback: If you have questions about any aspect of this book, email us at `customercare@packtpub.com` and mention the book title in the subject of your message.

Errata: Although we have taken every care to ensure the accuracy of our content, mistakes do happen. If you have found a mistake in this book, we would be grateful if you would report this to us. Please visit `www.packtpub.com/support/errata` and fill in the form.

Piracy: If you come across any illegal copies of our works in any form on the internet, we would be grateful if you would provide us with the location address or website name. Please contact us at `copyright@packt.com` with a link to the material.

If you are interested in becoming an author: If there is a topic that you have expertise in and you are interested in either writing or contributing to a book, please visit `authors.packtpub.com`

Share Your Thoughts

Once you've read *Business Process Automation with Salesforce Flows*, we'd love to hear your thoughts!
Scan the QR code below to go straight to the Amazon review page for this book and share your feedback.

https://packt.link/r/1835089259

Your review is important to us and the tech community and will help us make sure we're delivering
excellent quality content.

Download a free PDF copy of this book

Thanks for purchasing this book!

Do you like to read on the go but are unable to carry your print books everywhere?
Is your eBook purchase not compatible with the device of your choice?

Don't worry, now with every Packt book you get a DRM-free PDF version of that book at no cost.

Read anywhere, any place, on any device. Search, copy, and paste code from your favorite technical books directly into your application.

The perks don't stop there, you can get exclusive access to discounts, newsletters, and great free content in your inbox daily

Follow these simple steps to get the benefits:

1. Scan the QR code or visit the link below

https://packt.link/free-ebook/9781835089255

2. Submit your proof of purchase
3. That's it! We'll send your free PDF and other benefits to your email directly

Part 1: Understanding Business Requirements and Automation Needs

In this part, you will learn and understand the business requirements and the need for automating them so that the system can take care of the repetitive, redundant, and automatable tasks in the backend. We will explore and see how we can take advantage of tools that we can leverage and identify these tasks that can be automated. At the end of this part, you will be able to create a functional design specification that you can use to identify what tasks shall be performed by the end users and what tasks can be automated.

We will also address some of the key challenges faced during this phase:

- Not being able to identify the right set of requirements that can be automated.

- Lack of understanding of business needs and hence not being able to create a solution / design for what to and what not to automate.

- Too much automation is due to a lack of planning.

- Not assessing the impact of existing and planned automation holistically, resulting in automation logic executing randomly.

The following chapters will be covered in this part.

- *Chapter 1, Process Flows – Understanding Business Requirements*

- *Chapter 2, Identification of Functional Requirements for Automation*

- *Chapter 3, Business Process Features to Automate*

1

Process Flows – Understanding Business Requirements

In this chapter, we will explore and understand documented requirements and process flows. Only after a good understanding of business requirements and process steps can we confidently move to the next step to determine if a process step can be a potential candidate for automation. So, this chapter and the next chapter solely focus on aspects around understanding requirements and process flow steps.

We will assume that requirements are accurately captured and prioritized and that process flows are effectively developed. You can find details on these topics in *Chapters 1* and *2* of *The Salesforce Business Analyst Handbook*. In the event that your implementation of requirements and/or process flows is not clearly understood by all, make sure to clarify this before even thinking about automating your business processes.

Our focus in this book is to automate business processes, and this can be best done by first understanding business requirements in conjunction with process flow diagrams. We need a common understanding by identifying key stakeholders, SMEs, project team members, relevant tools and techniques, and collaboratively identifying and understanding requirements holistically, not just potential requirements that can be automated.

We will cover the following topics in this chapter:

- Types of business requirements
- Identifying the right stakeholders from project teams and SMEs
- Techniques and tools to identify requirements
- Understanding "as-is" and "to-be" business process flows
- Use-case scenario 1 – Partner user onboarding process
- Use-case scenario 2 – Quote approval process
- Tips for success

By the end of this chapter, you will understand business requirements with the aid of process flows. Process flows aid us in understanding business scenarios end to end with who does what, when, and how.

> **Note**
>
> Understanding business requirements is a must for any project role, be it admins, architects, designers, developers, testers, or any other stakeholder. Elicitation and documenting business needs and requirements may primarily rest with the business analyst on the project, but without all other team members understanding what the business needs are, this will jeopardize your implementation.

Types of business requirements

As an analyst on the project, our goal is to completely understand the full scope and intent of the business needs. By understanding different types of requirements, you will be able to manage the requirements process effectively at all project stages. Remind yourself that we are here to understand the requirements and end-to-end steps for the process so that we get to know the real problem or hidden opportunity and not to provide our opinions or solutions on what to or what not to automate. To understand this in greater detail, take a look at the *Identifying requirements* section of *The Salesforce Business Analyst Handbook*.

Let's look at the four main types of software requirements:

- **Business requirements**: These requirements describe the high-level functionality that the business needs. All stakeholders and anyone even remotely associated with the project should know and understand business requirements. The main purpose of the project is to provide a tool to streamline and automate the requirements to a certain extent.

  Example: Enable quote management for our channel partner **business unit** (BU).

- **Stakeholder requirements**: Features and functions the user needs and how they interact with the system. These system requirements translate into high-level step-by-step process flows.

  Example: All users will be able to access quote functionality via mobile devices.

- **System requirements**: These requirements describe the characteristics of the solution. We need to understand this level of granularity to determine and identify candidates for automation – for now, or in the future.

  Example: Based on the quote amount and account type, we need three levels of quote approval.

- **Transition requirements**: These are one-time requirements while moving from one system or process to another. Since they are not repetitive in nature, we do not need to worry much about them. Remember – if you have a multi-release roadmap, then you may need a few automated tools/scripts to reuse and simplify processes.

  Example: Data migration from legacy systems to new systems.

Knowing and understanding different types of requirements and establishing goals and timelines for identifying requirements will pave a solid foundation for the design, development, and testing phase of your project as well as help us to understand steps in business process flows.

Stakeholders from your project team and SMEs are the best sources of information. They may not explicitly understand business needs (this is where we need you), but they are certainly aware of problems and pain points. In the next section, you will find a quick overview of how to identify and involve our stakeholders so that business requirements can be understood effectively.

Identifying the right stakeholders from project teams and SMEs

One key success factor for any project is to be able to understand business requirements as well as business process flows. This can be accomplished only by involving the right set of users from the start of the project. The project team may be able to get some level of detail from past projects or implementation artifacts, but nothing beats the knowledge from key stakeholders and your end users who run the business.

The following are some tested ways that can help you in identifying and involving these key members:

- Your project **RACI** (short for **Responsible, Accountable, Consulted, and Informed**) matrix will help you identify stakeholders and SMEs. Make sure you pick the right set of users and not all stakeholders and SMEs. For our task, we need experts in their domain and users who potentially benefit from the project.

> Note
>
> A **RACI matrix** is a document that helps clarify who is responsible for the completion of project tasks and the roles individuals or groups play during the project. Every project should have a RACI matrix that defines project responsibilities on a project. Anyone related to the project will know their role and responsibilities, as well as those of other team members.

- Most of the time, some very knowledgeable SMEs and highly skilled stakeholders may not be on the project. Make sure you reach out to the program management team and project sponsor and get their help in engaging these valuable resources. It may not be possible for these users to join all the **conference room pilots** (**CRPs**) or workshops; it will greatly help us if we can meet them offline and get their input/feedback. CRPs are workshops where key stakeholders, along with project team members, collaborate at various stages of projects to understand the business needs while transforming them into proposed business solutions.

- Do your homework and involve the right stakeholder who is relevant to a specific session. If your session is around lead management, there is no point in involving an expert from quote or contract management. Be cognizant of their time; this is very important as they have their regular job to perform.

- Keep an eye on stakeholders' conflicting priorities. Things may sometimes get out of control if ground rules are not set. You need to have an established conflict escalation and resolution mechanism. If not, some stakeholders may lose interest or may skip future sessions altogether.

- After each session, make sure you send the minutes of that meeting, along with visuals such as the process flow chart that was discussed during the session, and solicit feedback. This helps ideas discussed during the meeting crystallize, and if something pops into stakeholders' heads, it will be a bonus for the project team.

- Make a list of stakeholders by session and understand them well in advance. Get to know their strengths, influences, likes, dislikes, hobbies, and so on. This will help you manage the sessions productively. Always make sure you know them by their name.

- Make sure you reach out to the end users; these are the users who perform the tasks every day. They may not be able to articulate confidently or freely. Discuss the project with them in one-on-one breakout sessions and get to know what they have to say. You will find nuggets of wisdom, and they can be game-changers.

Identifying and involving key stakeholders (such as your project sponsor, business SMEs, superusers, compliance, software vendors, and enterprise architects) and end users during a conversation helps get everyone on the same page. Most importantly, this group can help identify the true business needs and the way the business runs.

> **Note**
>
> Do not assume anything when it comes to business requirements. It's as simple as this – the business wants it or does not want it. So, clarify your understanding and make sure everyone on the team has the same understanding. All assumptions need to be agreed upon by all stakeholders and properly documented.

Techniques and tools to identify requirements

In the previous section, we successfully identified key stakeholders, SMEs, and end users who can add tremendous value in identifying and explaining their business needs and business processes. Now, the question is: *How to get this valuable information from these users?*

Elicitation is a method to draw out business needs and requirements. To effectively do so, we usually use a combination of these techniques that best fit your organization's culture. Some of these elicitation techniques are observation, brainstorming, CRPs, prototyping, process models, and user stories.

All projects have finite resources, and we need to prioritize an unending list of requirements so that we can deliver the most value to the business. There are proven and effective techniques to prioritize requirements. Some of them are the MoSCoW method, weighted ranking, SWOT analysis, story mapping, and so on. Prioritizing is an important activity to set expectations via a project release roadmap with your stakeholders and your user community.

All these techniques and methods can help only if they are communicated, collaborated on, and managed. So, this is where your soft skills will come into play. You need to understand your stakeholders, plan and communicate meetings/sessions well in advance, prepare and plan your conversations, tailor the conversation to match participants' styles, listen actively, ask the right questions, structure your conversation, take notes, use visuals, provide and solicit feedback, and finally, make sure to thank them for helping your team understand the project needs.

Techniques, tools, and skills help us get to a list of prioritized requirements. There may still be gaps and missed opportunities within this prioritized list. Also, not every team member – especially your design, development, and testing team members – may understand where these requirements fit in the grand scheme of business. We will explore this in the next section.

Understanding "as-is" and "to-be" business process flows

Different stakeholders and project team members can see and interpret a requirement from their perspective and understand it very differently. To overcome these very issues, business process flows/charts come to our rescue. Process flows can be high-level and get to extremely detailed levels. Too complex, and you will lose the business user; too easy, and the design and development team will miss critical steps in the process. Process flows are iterative, and they start small and get complex. We need to strike a balance and get to one that aids common understanding among all participants.

During the requirements-gathering phase of the project, your project team, especially the business analyst, works with key stakeholders to understand the current process. Before the project, the business users may be doing all the process steps manually in multiple systems; still, it is a business process step from start to finish. After we have the finalized requirements, we will be able to create a future state process flow and, along the way, identify any gaps or opportunities in the process.

There are three distinct process flows that are important for most projects:

- **Macro process maps**: These provide a very high-level view for management and the entire team.
- **Business process flows**: The "as-is" is also called the current state, and the "to-be" is called the future state. We are more interested in this process flow and will be referring to this in this book.
- **Architectural process flows**: These are complex and highly technical, with all sorts of cross-functional integrations. These flows are very helpful for your technical team as well as your integration teams.

In the next section, we will visit two simplified real-world business process flow scenarios.

Projects can be very simple to extremely complex. Let's take two scenarios – moderately simple and complex implementations – and see how to understand the requirements. Again, remember that our goal here is to understand the business requirements, and we need this knowledge to get into the next stage and help us identify requirements steps that can potentially be automated (partially or entirely).

Let us look at two simplified scenarios. These use cases are very complex; for the sake of simplicity and understanding, they are greatly simplified so that you get the gist of business process flows.

Use-case scenario 1 – Partner user onboarding process

In this first scenario, I will walk you through the **Partner Relationship Management** (**PRM**) partner user onboarding process. The flow is for a partner user to request access and be able to get access to your Salesforce PRM system and access channel sales functionality.

> **Note**
>
> **PRM** – aka **channel sales** – is a tool that helps companies/organizations manage their partners. PRM helps manage relationships and interactions between your sales team and your partners— retailers, distributors, systems integrators, referral partners, **managed service providers** (**MSPs**), and so on.

Before this project, the registration process was performed in multiple systems, including many manual processes. The business requirements are to enable PRM for partner users in Salesforce in a multi-release roadmap.

Let us look at some business requirements (partner registration) at a high level. During the initial CRP session, we can get these requirements so that we can use them as a starting point to create a conceptual process flow (with more iterations, we will get to the final process flow for the project):

1. Partner users will be able to request registrations to your organization.
2. Channel team members will be able to use PRM functionality (separate complex business requirements to enable partner accounts, deal registration, opportunity management, **marketing development funds** (**MDF**), and quote and contract management functions).
3. The sales operations team will be able to create/update partner accounts and contact data.
4. System admins will be able to convert partner contacts into partner users using PRM user licenses.

Based on these high-level requirements, your business analysts should have created a process flow with the help of project stakeholders, SMEs, and solution architects, as shown in *Figure 1.1* with the partner registration simplified process flow diagram.

This process takes us through typical partner registration requests, starting with registration requests from partners and going through multiple steps before finally getting approved.

The high-level steps in the partner registration business process are set out here:

1. The partner (channel partner) requests registration in your PRM system to access the Salesforce system and collaborate with your sales team.
2. The channel team receives a registration request from partners.

3. A review process is involved before you can proceed with this information.

4. The next step is requesting sales operations to create account and contact records.

5. Sales operations create an account and contact and request that the admin provisions the user.

6. The admin creates a partner user.

7. The process ends after creating a partner user record:

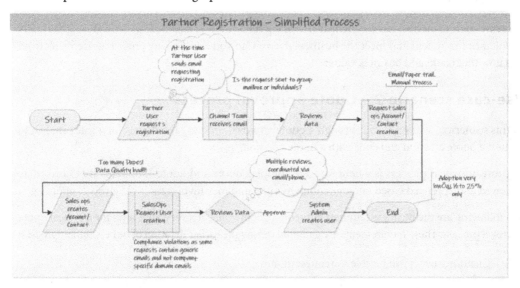

Figure 1.1 – Partner registration: simplified process

This kind of simplified process flow will help everyone on the project, including stakeholders, project team members, and end users, understand the process very succinctly. This process flow takes a few iterations before it takes shape into a fully-fledged process flow. This is collaboratively developed involving all the right team members as part of your business analysis activities involving elicitation and documenting requirements.

Once you have the business flow from end to end agreed upon by all the key stakeholders in iterative workshops or CRPs, the team will be able to identify requirements at a more granular level. At this time, focus on understanding the flow rather than judging what can be automated. Remember – complete automation may take a few releases or the project sponsor may decide that only key repetitive tasks should be automated due to budget or time constraints. So, our goal is to focus on identifying all the requirements and any gaps in the process flows.

If we look closely at the process, we will be able to identify gaps/requirements, such as the following:

1. How does the partner user send the request? How are changes to the original request handled?

2. Does the request get to individuals? What happens if the individual is not with the organization anymore?

3.   Duplicate records are most common in legacy systems. How do we avoid duplicate data?

4.   The aforementioned process only tells us to grant access. Do all partner users get to see all of the partner functionality, or is it based on certain attributes? *Example*: Only platinum partners get to request and avail of MDF.

5.   We can see that SMEs and end users stated that adoption is very low. What are the pain points, and how can we improve this?

These are some of the business requirements. Looking at the low user adoption, we see a great opportunity to enhance the system and meet the business needs. Can you think of any other requirements from this flow that could add business value?

Use-case scenario 2 – Quote approval process

In this scenario, I will walk you through a quote approval process. The flow is for a sales analyst to request a quote creation and ends with a quote creation.

A **quote approval process** is where we have complex quote and quote-line items that need to be reviewed and approved based on your company rules and may involve multiple levels of approval.

The following are the business requirements (quote approvals) at a very high level for a typical quote approval process. These requirements are gathered during the earlier iteration of our elicitation process:

1.   Customer users will be able to request quotes.

2.   The deal team will be able to review and create a quote and add products to the quote.

3.   The deal team will be able to apply discounts based on customer tier, volume, and product family.

4.   The deal team will be able to attach supplemental documents such as PDF, Excel, PowerPoint files, and so on during the quote creation process.

5.   Quote approvals are required based on attributes such as total amount and for certain product groups.

6.   Ability to send the finalized quote to the customer.

For these requirements let's check the conceptual process flow developed by your project team in *Figure 1.2*:

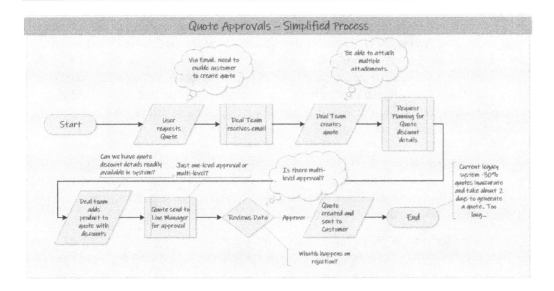

Figure 1.2 – Quote approvals: simplified process

The preceding quote approval flow helps CRP participants understand the quote creation as well as approval steps in the process from start to end. Again, creating a process flow starts simple and gets complex as team members understand the process better. From the process flow, some of the queries around requirements are listed next:

1. Can the sales analyst request a quote from the system?

2. What notification is required, and can the analyst see the progress?

3. Can the deal team access the discount matrix while creating the quote? (Complex rules for applying discounts based on account tier, product family, and so on.)

4. What percentage of quotes need multi-level approval? (This query will help us tag this as a potential item for automation, which will be discussed in later chapters.)

5. How do we send the quote to the customer? Is it alright to send a PDF quote to the customer?

6. How can we reduce the end-to-end quote cycle?

These queries are raised by different participants but are collectively discussed to get the same understanding. Not all queries may make sense, but this is the right place for your team to discuss them and confirm. The finer the details you can elicit, the better it will be for the next phase of your projects.

I hope the preceding two scenarios provided you with a good idea of how your team will be able to understand the steps and hence the requirements behind these process steps. There are many tools that you can use to create process flows, such as **Business Process Modelling Notation** (**BPMN**), Flowchart, Lucidchart, Visio, **Unified Modeling Language** (**UML**) diagrams, and so on. If you do not have access to these tools, simply use a whiteboard and then capture the same on your mobile device.

No matter what your role is in the project, always try to understand the business requirements and the business process flow. Reading the requirements in conjunction with process flows will help understand the requirements with clarity. You must make every effort to understand business needs and wants, how they align with the vision and strategy, and how this enables us to achieve our strategic end goal. To understand business needs, you need to understand how they are operated. Understanding the current process and what will be the desired future state is important so that you can find the right solution and fulfill business needs.

Tips for success

- Get to know the project stakeholders, SMEs, and project team members. You can get info from organization charts and social profiles.

- If you are a business analyst, you will probably be facilitating and documenting these requirements and process flows. If you are not, make sure you are involved during these discussions.

- Make sure to encourage everyone to contribute and ask questions. This will help everyone on the team. This includes you too.

- Send minutes of the meeting by the end of the day to all participants. Follow up as needed till you and the stakeholders understand and agree to high-level requirements.

- Do not get into designing solutions. Understand the business requirements and process flows. Remember – you do not yet know what requirements will be in scope. Your goal should be to gain a good understanding of the complete situation and not provide options or solutions.

- Approach the project with a design-thinking mindset. Look for people and their needs before feasibility and viability to maximize usability and user experience.

- Actively listen, encourage, and engage participants to freely collaborate, take notes, manage conflicts, and keep the meeting on track.

Summary

In this chapter, we discussed ways to identify the right project participants and then checked which tools and techniques there are to help us understand the business requirements. You now understand the importance of business process flows for common understanding by the entire project team with simplified real-world scenarios. We ended the chapter with a few tips for success.

In the next chapter, we discuss functional requirements and see if they make a good case for automation. We will look at an example **functional specification document** (**FSD**) with a few real-world scenarios.

Questions

1. What do we capture in a process flow and what is an "as-is" process flow?

2. Do all project team members need to understand business requirements? Why?

3. Name a few tools that you can use to create business process flows.

4. What is a RACI matrix?

Further reading

- *Srini Munagavalasa. The Salesforce Business Analyst Handbook, Part 1: Planning and Analysis. Packt Publishing Ltd (2022).*

- *IIBA. A Guide to the Business Analysis Body of Knowledge. Lightning Source Inc (2015).*

2

Identification of Functional Requirements for Automation

In the last chapter, we reviewed ways to understand business requirements using business process flows. We primarily used these flows to identify high-level business requirements during the pre-planning and/or planning phase of your project. During the design phase of the projects, these high-level product requirements will generate more granular and refined requirements, also called **functional** and **non-functional requirements**.

In this chapter, we will cover solution design aspects of functional requirements. We will explore in detail how to split requirements into tasks that can be automated. We will dive deep and discuss the rationale for every task that we intend to automate.

We will cover the following topics in this chapter:

- What are functional requirements?
- Identifying functional tasks that can be automated
- Developing a **functional specification document** (**FSD**) outlining tasks to be automated
- Practical tips for success

By the end of this chapter, you will understand business requirements with the aid of process flows. Process flows aid us in understanding business scenarios end to end with who does what, when, and how.

> **Note**
> **Requirements evolution**: Requirements evolution starts with business/product requirements and then evolves into more detailed user or stakeholder requirements, and progressively gets into more detailed functional and technical requirements.

What are functional requirements?

Functional requirements describe a specific set of capabilities that a system must provide to users to achieve their goals. These are the actions that users would like to perform so that they can achieve the desired business needs or expectations. A functional requirement states how a system must behave to meet users' needs; it can be capabilities that users perform or capabilities that the system performs without users' intervention. We need to understand and capture what the system does (function) and how the system does it (behavior) while documenting functional requirements. For more details on functional requirements, check out *Chapter 5, Business Requirements Documents*, of *The Salesforce Business Analyst Handbook*.

At this point, we are trying to understand all the functional aspects of the requirements. Let us focus on understanding all functional requirements. At a minimum, we need to be able to understand the business requirements and be able to deliver **MVP** (short for **minimum viable product**) functionality so that our business users can start using the features at the earliest possible opportunity. They are looking at functionality, not automation. Automation may not always add value during the initial stages, and as your organization grows, automation may become more relevant.

These are the assumptions with the requirements we have so far during the planning phase of the project:

1. We do not know the scope of functional requirements yet.
2. We do not know if we have enough resources to automate.
3. Even if we know what we automate, we do not know which automation tools to use yet.

Let us look at a few examples of functional requirements:

- Users (sales analysts, sales managers, and sales operations users) will be able to generate quotes from opportunity records and be able to create quote line items
- The user (sales analyst) will be able to apply regular discounts at quote line items, and the discount percentage should not exceed 10% for product group A and 15% for product group B
- Users (sales managers and sales operations users) will be able to modify quotes and apply additional discounts
- Users will get approval from the finance team if the discount amount is greater than 25% or if the quoted amount before the discount is greater than 100K USD
- Only sales operations users will be able to convert account types from Prospect to Customer and associate customer **KYC** (short for **Know Your Customer**) IDs

> **Note**
>
> Non-functional requirements are important for the overall project's success, but we will not be covering them as they are not critical for automation. We will focus on automating functional requirements so that you can get the core concepts.

Identifying functional tasks that can be automated

In the previous section, we reviewed the functional requirements for our project. Functional requirements are then prioritized and grouped into various releases as per the project roadmap during the project planning phase. In this section, we will explore and see which functional specifications can be potentially automated.

Always remember that during the initial releases, enabling functionality for users involving manual steps is more desirable than spending valuable project resources on designing and developing automation. These very steps that are performed manually during initial releases can be automated in future releases based on usage and user feedback. I personally found this approach highly effective with my project implementations.

But exactly what is **business process automation (BPA)**? BPA is software-enabled automation that automates multistep, repetitive tasks with little or no human intervention. In this book, we will focus on BPA using Flow Builder. Many times, integrations get very complex and span across multiple software systems. In that case, some examples of other BPA tools that can be used are Dataloader.io, Salesforce (MuleSoft), IBM App Connect, and Oracle Self-Service Integration.

Automating everything will create a bland user experience for your users. You need to let your users interact with the system sufficiently so that it creates a lively feeling—not too little or not too much. To give you context, look at IKEA furniture; they do not sell ready-to-use furniture; rather, they sell designs and ready-to-assemble furniture. You get the furniture, spend a few hours reading the step-by-step instructions, and assemble the furniture on your own. This creates a feeling that you made the product and take pride in the product. This is one of the secrets of IKEA's success.

The best way to identify all tasks is by breaking down the functionality of the business process into easily understood steps called **scenarios**. These scenarios are revisited iteratively with all the right stakeholders before they can be agreed upon. The best approach I take is to create a process flow and document all these steps with a rationale for each step: why do we need this task and how does it aid our business?

> **Note**
>
> When you plan your automation, make sure to strike a balance between what users should be doing and what the system should do to make the experience interactive. Too much makes the users interact with the system less, and they may not get the complete picture. Too little or no automation will create redundancy and duplicity.

Let us revisit each of the previously identified functional specifications and see whether they can be automated (remember—just because something can be automated does not mean it should be automated):

1. **User (sales analyst, sales manager, sales operations users) will be able to generate quotes from opportunity records and be able to create quote line items**: This is a straightforward functional requirement, and no automation is required unless you have complex opportunity management with custom fields and multiple discount attributes. Anything that can be easily done by a small set of users should not be prioritized for automation. New functionality should be prioritized before any automation.

2. **The user (sales analyst) will be able to apply regular discounts at quote line items and the discount percent should not exceed 10% for product group A and 15% for product group B**: A discount percentage here is optional. The sales analyst will be able to apply a discount up to a maximum of 10% for product group A and 15% for product group B. Based on the product group, we can think of automating a default discount percentage for each quote product line item based on which product group they belong to.

   We have two scenarios to consider here:

   A. Discounts are provided rarely, so if we automate and default, the analyst may forget to remove the discount, and if accidentally applied to many quotes, it will impact our bottom line.

   B. Discounts are very frequently applied, so defaulting makes sense so that the right discount percentage is applied.

   This is a viable candidate for automation during a future release after getting feedback during the initial release. The discount matrix is more complex, and automating makes sense when calculations are involved. Also, automating this will help us with any human errors and incorrect discounts on quotes.

3. **Users (sales manager, sales operations users) will be able to modify quotes and be able to apply additional discounts**: The sales manager/sales operations and not the sales analyst can modify the quote to apply an additional discount. Since this is done by a small set of users and additional discount is discretionary, we do not need any automation. But if additional discounts depend on the account type, product family group, customer region, and so on, then we need to explore and see if the process can be automated.

4. **Users will get approval from the finance team if the discount amount is greater than 25% or if the quoted amount before the discount is greater than 100K USD**: I am sure we should automate the process. This automation needs notification and a workflow approval process. The aforementioned functional requirement is too simplified, but you will have a distinct set of approvers and multi-level approval processes. It would be beneficial if this could be automated in the same release as the functionality. Also, this may be potentially approved by a senior team member due to the value of the quoted amount. We need to automate this as senior members are busy and they may have too many tasks on their plate.

5. **Only sales operations users will be able to convert account types from Prospect to Customer and be able to associate customer KYC IDs**: This certainly is not required to be automated. The users are only sales operations, who can perform this activity of converting an account from Prospect to Customer, but they also need the KYC ID. KYC is a complex process, and this functionality can reside in the same system or a completely different system. So, we will not plan to automate as we will let sales operations get the KYC ID and add it to the system while converting the account.

These are some of the examples, and I hope you got an idea. We do not automate just because the system is capable. You need to consider how it is useful to the business—usability, user engagement, resource availability, value addition, and so on.

Process flows such as the ones we discussed in *Chapter 1* will come in very handy. We can superimpose these requirements on the process flow and trace all the steps needed to fulfill the functional requirement. Now, let's check and see if each step of the process makes a suitable candidate for system automation.

Developing an FSD outlining tasks to be automated

In this section, we will briefly look at an FSD and decide which steps of the specification can be automated. Identifying these upfront in the FSD will help not only the technical team to build the functionality and automation, but also set expectations with the business users. Socializing this with all key stakeholders will help form a collective understanding of the requirement and how it will be performed. Sometimes, what we think needs to be automated may not be agreeable to the business stakeholders. This is good to know beforehand, and resources can be better utilized for other requirements.

How to create an FSD is not in the scope of this book. In this section, we will take a quick look at typical CRM functional design document fields that are important.

Typical FSD fields are listed next. Notice the *Can be automated?* and *Estimated effort* columns in the following table. This will help us to identify if the functional steps need to be automated, either now or in the future. Whether you use Agile or waterfall project methodology, we need the functional specification and a visual process flow for any requirements. This is more important if you plan to automate the steps. If you cannot draw it visually, you should not automate it. Automating steps without common stakeholder understanding causes more frustration and confusion. You should be able to document any requirement in more than one way – functional specification, use case, or flow charts. No matter how we describe the requirements, they should all convey the same meaning to all your project stakeholders:

FSD: Excel document with the following columns	
Business requirements document (BRD) ID (unique ID)	`<Function Name>-<NN>` – for example, `Account-01`.
Purpose	The business objective of a requirement.
BRD summary	A requirement summary in simple business language.

FSD ID	You can use any unique identifier; the best practice is to concatenate FS, BRD ID, and NN since one BRD can have multiple FSD line items – for example: FS- Account-01.01, FS- Account-01, 02…., FS- Account-01.10.
FSD summary	Summary of requirements in more technical terms so that the technical team understands exactly the steps in the business requirements.
FSD details	It includes granular details that your technical team can understand. Process flows will help you capture these details more accurately.
Normal flow	This is the most optimistic flow. This is what the user does to achieve their goal when no issues are encountered – a happy path.
Alternative flow	If the user encounters issues, provide steps for them to take a different flow.
Exception flow	In the event of an error, this will be the system response.
Business rule	Capture business rules associated with a requirement. For example, account records cannot be converted from Prospect to Customer without a KYC ID.
User actions	The steps the users perform in the system – for example, logging in to Salesforce, accessing the Account tab, clicking on Create new records, entering all the required fields, and successfully saving the record.
System response	The system displays a human-understandable success, error, or information message.
Complexity (H/M/L)	High, medium, or low.
Can be automated?	Yes/no.
Estimated effort	Capture estimates with and without automation. This will give us an idea if we should or should not automate this step of the functional specification.
Phase of project	Phases such as Release –1, Release –2, Release –3, and so on.
Documented date	The date when a requirement is added to a matrix.
In/out scope	Your prioritized list usually consists of approved in-scope items; in some cases, due to technical limitations or resource constraints, you can defer a few requirements to future releases. Here, you can tag the deferred ones as out of scope.
Comments	Add any comments or details that add clarity to your requirement.

This is a comprehensive list of key sections in functional documents. As needed, add other relevant sections that you think add value to your implementation. As with BRD, you review this with technical and testing leads and SMEs, get agreement and approval from all, and lock this document. You should share this document with business SMEs and stakeholders so that they can review and provide input. However, their approval may be optional. This baseline version will be your starting document for subsequent releases on your roadmap.

Practical tips for success

Here are a few practical tips for success:

- The functional document should also address the **user interface** (**UI**) and usability of the application for better user adoption. As needed, it will be beneficial to mock up the screen's navigation, look, and feel in the FSD.

- When trying to automate integrations that process large data volumes, think through and see how you want to automate it. Large volumes of data and the complexity of the requirements can put a spin on automation and severely impact the performance of your automation.

- Capture details on how well any system or data exception is handled and logged.

- Doing functional document peer reviews before getting it signed off helps make it a complete document.

- Your process flows should be system agnostic, and not all steps can be implemented and/or automated in one release. A manual process in one release can be an automated process in a future release.

- Collaborate and create process flows with input from key team members. All members should be on board with the overall solution design before actual development work is started.

- The functional document is the main point of reference document for the technical and testing teams. Make sure enough details are captured, if possible, in technical terms.

Summary

In this chapter, we discussed functional requirements with examples. Then, we expanded each of these functional requirements into steps and studied if they can be automated now or at a future date. Finally, we concluded the chapter with key attributes that make up a good FSD.

In the next chapter, we will explore effort requirements and how to add value incrementally to your business. You will be able to learn methods to identify tasks that can be automated that are important and provide business value.

Questions

1. When do you prioritize automating steps in your business process flows?
2. What is BPA?
3. Think of a few automations that are beneficial to your projects.

Further reading

- *Srini Munagavalasa (2022). The Salesforce Business Analyst Handbook – Chapter 6, Solution Design and Functional Document. Packt Publishing Ltd.*

- *Suzanne Robertson, James Robertson (2012). Mastering the Requirements Process: Getting Requirements Right, 3rd Edition. Addison-Wesley Professional.*

3
Business Process Features to Automate

In the last chapter, we reviewed functional requirements with examples. We expanded these functional requirements into steps and analyzed them for potential automation. We visited a typical set of fields that make up a good functional specification document.

In this chapter, you will discuss why it is important to allocate enough time and prioritize requirements automation. Prioritizing does not mean bringing requirements to the top as they come in from business users, but rather distributing around different releases on the roadmap to add optimum value to the overall business. You will be able to learn methods to identify important tasks and provide business value.

We will cover the following topics in this chapter:

- Automation tools available in Salesforce
- Identifying potential automation steps
- Scenarios – Rationale for automation
- Getting consensus and agreement from all stakeholders
- Practical tips on prioritizing requirements

By the end of this chapter, you will understand business process features to automate and time them in such a way that gives maximum benefit to the project and our business users.

> **Note**
>
> Requirements keep evolving and get refined until the end of the design phase, assuming business analysis work is performed effectively. Once key stakeholders understand their asks (the business need and any assumptions around the need) after iterative discussions during various workshops and prototypes, this will solidify into complete requirements. In a few cases, the original requirements may completely evolve into different requirements from the original business need. This helps us not to develop and deploy unwanted functionality concerning the invalid requirement.
>
> A valid requirement may evolve into an invalid requirement at a future date based on factors such as changes in business processes, operating environmental factors, changes in stakeholders, and so on.

Automation tools available in Salesforce

Automation does not mean we need to use fancy tools; if we can reduce steps in any process by any way or means, that can qualify as automation (or partial automation). Say you can enable users to capture data on one screen rather than do it on multiple tabs with multiple clicks – this is automation. A good example is the **Salesforce Console**.

Let us see which automation features and tools we have in Salesforce. The chapters from *Part 2* entirely focus on Salesforce flows, but before we get there, I would like to show you all the great features and functions we can use to automate our functional requirements in Salesforce.

Broadly, we have the following tools to automate in Salesforce. Let's look at each one of them to get an idea of what automation means:

- **Formula fields**: These help us with automated calculations based on defined formulas. They are quick and easy to create and useful for users of the page layouts. These fields are calculated dynamically and are not stored in the database. We cannot use them in report filters or list views.

- **Dependent picklist**: To limit the list of values in one picklist based on another picklist values. *Example*: We would like to display a list of products based on the Product family. (Product is a dependent picklist on the Product family.) Similarly, we want to display Product families based on the selected Product group. (Product Family is a dependent picklist on Product Group.) By creating dependencies, we can restrict the list of records the user can choose. There are a few considerations, such as **Field-Level Security** (**FLS**) settings for a controlling field and dependent picklists are independent. Also, the Data Import Wizard does not consider field dependencies.

- **Roll-up summaries**: For objects with master-detail relationships, the roll-up summary field calculates values from related records. *Example*: Count of all opportunities on an account; the sum of the amount of all product opportunities on an opportunity. It is a great automation feature, but it works only on objects that have a master-detail relationship.

- **Flows** (since **Workflow Actions** and **Process Builder** are deprecated, we will not cover them): An automation tool on steroids to automate business processes with click and low code. This book is all about flows.

- **Outbound messages**: This is a workflow approval action that sends information to an external server. An outbound message sends information to a designated endpoint, such as external services. *Example*: When an account owner or address changes on your customer record, we can generate by triggering an outbound API message to an external KYC system to reflect the right data. This feature allows us to transmit data via API message to external systems in **SOAP** (short for **Simple Object Access Protocol**) format.

- **Approval process**: This is a type of reliable, repeatable, and well-structured automated business process with a series of steps to validate, review, and approve or reject tasks based on predetermined business rules. *Example*: Customer quotes need multi-level approval based on $ amount.

- **Apex triggers**: This is our pro-code automation solution. Where other methods fail, this is the best tool. You should opt for pro-code if your business processes are highly complex and if you have excellent in-house technical skills. Also, flows cannot be used for certain scenarios, such as complex list processing or custom validation errors.

- **Salesforce AppExchange products**: Plugin products that are seamlessly integrated with Salesforce are another great integration option. The integration is seamless, and they are plug-and-play. *Examples*: D&B Connect, LinkedIn Sales Solutions, Conga Composer, and so on.

- **External third-party tools**: Tools such as Informatica, MuleSoft, and Splunk are high-level integration tools. For complex projects, probably use these and other tools.

> **Note**
>
> Flows can use one or more of the other types of automation from Flow Builder (a tool to build flows). As an example, we can call approval processes from flows. Understanding automation tools in Salesforce is very important.

These are the main tools we can use to enable automation. Based on the business requirements and project dynamics at your organization, your team can pick the one that meets your needs. A simple example will be to use the roll-up summary field to calculate the sum, count, average, minimum, or maximum for currency, number, and date fields. This makes sense if you want to roll up the amount field from all products onto your opportunity. What if there is no master-detail relationship between objects or if we want the roll-up data further calculated and available on the child record? Similarly, if we have a requirement to calculate values based on other fields, formula fields are no-brainers. What if we need this formula field in short for **List View Controls** (**LVCs**) and reports? Can we still do it using formula fields or do we need to adopt another way?

There are many ways to automate tasks, and which way you pick depends on many factors for that point in time. For smaller implementations, you may not even need any automation as the business users are focused on getting some secure system to run the business with basic out-of-the-box features such as reports, dashboards, LSVs, audit logs, and access controls.

Identifying potential automation steps

In the previous section, we checked various automation tools that are available in the Salesforce platform. With the right understanding of the Salesforce system, functional knowledge, and experience, you can perform miracles.

To enable this functionality in any IT system, we need to have the process understood and defined. Let's briefly see what a process model is and why it is important to understand it. For details, check *Chapter 4* of my book, *The Salesforce Business Analyst Handbook*.

Process models help us understand the current business processes "as-is," and future desired "to-be" processes.

We start with creating a high-level draft model, iteratively developing, refining, and transforming it as permanent artifacts using the tool of your choice. I prefer to use the **Visio** tool to create a process flow and then socialize the Visio process flows in PDF format to stakeholders and get their feedback and agreement.

At each step in the process, collaboratively discuss and check with the workshop participants:

- How to simplify this step in the process flow?

- Do we automate a specific step? Does it make sense?

- Intuitive screen flow design that guides the users along the process

- Can we provide the user with a complete picture, such as a 360-degree view of the account?

Using a flowchart, we can communicate complex processes in a clear, understandable format with our stakeholders and improve business processes. There are many other models available to capture process flows; it is best to use the one you are most comfortable with. These are a few process flow models that we can use to develop our process model:

- **Flowcharts**: Flowcharts are diagrams that graphically represent a process in a sequence of steps and decision-making points. They are useful for less complex flows. Using a flowchart, we can communicate complex processes in a clear, understandable format with our stakeholders and also improve business processes.

- **Business Process Modeling Notation (BPMN)**: BPMN is used to model business processes and is more advanced than flowcharts. BPMN is a flowchart method that allows teams to graphically capture and document business process flows and provide a clear view of a specific process in sequential steps from start to finish. BPMN flows enable us to clarify communication between different project stakeholders and aid in business process improvements.

- **Unified Modeling Language (UML) diagram**: UML diagrams are usually used to model software systems but can be used for process modeling. UML is a general-purpose modeling language that defines a standard way to visualize the designed system.

Let's look at a simplified process model and check if a specific process can be automated.

Scenarios – Rationale for automation

We will explore a real-world scenario in this section, starting with defining high-level requirements and going more granularly into low-level requirements. With the aid of a process flow, we will discuss the rationale behind the steps we plan to automate.

High-level requirement:

> The user will be able to request and gain access to accounts and related records such as contacts, opportunities, and cases. Users not within specific business groups need compliance approval before they can be granted access to the account and related records.

Low-level functional requirements:

1. The sales analyst requests access to Salesforce data.
2. The sales manager/sales operations will be able to add users to the account team.
3. Compliance needs to approve user access if they do not belong to the same group. *Example*: Sales users in Zone 1 can be granted access to any of the records owned by users from Zone 1, whereas if a Zone 2 user needs access to Zone 1 users' data, compliance approval is required.
4. Compliance reviews the request and can approve or reject the case.

Let's go through each step and see what can be automated and see if that makes sense:

1. Can the sales analyst request access directly from the system, by creating a case?
2. If a request conforms to the guidelines (which means users belong to the same sales group), can we automate account team creation on case approval by the sales manager/operations, or do they need to create an account team manually? This makes sense to automate, but do we have time and resources? What is the volume of users we have in our instance? If not a large volume, does it make sense to automate?
3. Is case management required? Or do we get approval outside the system?
4. Do we need to build approval processes if the data volume and frequency are low? Do we have licenses to the system for compliance users? Assuming you have good user bases and medium to high volume data, it makes sense to enable case management and automate account team creation. Here is the reason: We need cases available handy for auditing and automating account team creation to help compliance users.
5. Do we automate email notifications based on actions in the system, or is it done outside the system? Do the users need to be active in the system to be able to get notifications? Automating email notifications sounds like a no-brainer, but what if the users do not have access to the system and you need a response from the user, such as approve/reject?

6. Can we automate account team creation when the case is approved by compliance, or do they create or notify sales operations to create an account team?

7. Do we automate notifications to sales analysts after their access is approved/rejected? It makes sense to automate this as the users are in the system and it is just a simple notification.

Here is a process flow diagram for an account access request:

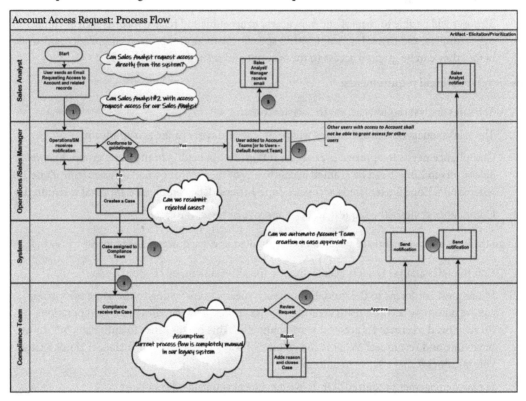

Figure 3.1 – Account access request: simplified process flow (Visio)

Review each step with the workshop participants and make sure you do that in a few iterations. Your business users can easily see clearly from the process flow if they do or do not need automation. Remember – at a later release, some of the manual steps may have to be automated at a future release for better adoption and business value addition. Say, for example, you have lots of requests around account access (additions and removals); it makes sense to automate the account team creation process when a case is approved. We have dual benefits here. During the initial release, we provided case management functionality. In the next release, we added approval process functionality, and finally, we added auto account team creation functionality. Adding features this way adds incremental values, and they can be added or skipped based on the user's feedback.

> **Note**
>
> If the same set of users needs similar access to data, the account owner will be able to add the user to the account team and sales team from their user record. This is a one-time process, and we can default on this team on all account teams and opportunity teams. If they are a different set of users, team members need to be added at the account/opportunity record level.

Now that we have identified the requirement in more detail and are able to assess if it adds value to automate all or some steps in the process, the next very important step is to socialize with all our key stakeholders and the project team and get a common understanding and agreement on the requirements as a whole, as well as potential tasks planned to be automated. Let's check this out in the next section.

Getting consensus and agreement from all stakeholders

In the last section, we got an opportunity to identify all the requirement steps – most importantly, the ones that can potentially be automated using a process flow diagram. I cannot emphasize enough how important these process flows are. If your team cannot draw your business process and explain it visually, that means you do not understand your business process completely, and this translates to incomplete requirements gathering and understanding of your business needs. If this is the case, take a pause and make sure requirements are elicited, documented, and agreed on by all project stakeholders. Make use of a whiteboard or a flip chart during your workshops, and develop the process flow with the help of your business stakeholders, SMEs, and project team members.

Here are some considerations to make an agreement with key stakeholders:

- **Be an active listener**: Be able to understand the meaning behind the work and the user's intentions.
- Understand the user needs in the context and be technology agnostic.
- Avoid stakeholders telling you what to do (solution) rather than what they need.
- Adopt incremental approaches where possible to foster innovative solutions and better solutions.
- Take notes… lots of them. Tag the source where you got the information. Later, if you need clarification, it helps you identify the source easily.
- Use visuals as much as possible to bring everyone to a common understanding.
- **Communicate**: Send the minutes to all stakeholders, including the visuals, and solicit feedback.

You can make prioritization meetings meaningful and effective, as follows:

- Engagement rules should be communicated
- Prioritization meetings should be well planned and communicated
- A clear agenda and goals should be communicated
- Ground rules for conflict resolution should be established

- Educate and give an overview of the tools and techniques the team plans to use

- Define criteria for prioritizing factors and their weights

- Set up a good conference room with a large wall-to-wall whiteboard, flip charts, and projector to display previously created process flows, conceptual flows, and so on

> **Note**
>
> Project teams do not define and create business process flows. We from the IT team do not tell the business users how to run their businesses. We help develop business process diagrams and fine-tune them with our key stakeholders and SMEs. However, the project team should discuss best practices and suggestions on how to improve the business processes. Ultimately, the business users in the workshop should consent or reject and they have the final say on what the business process should look like. Business process diagrams are reflections of your business processes, and they get refined iteratively many times during each release. We take a snapshot of the business process flow diagrams during each release so that we can use them as a baseline for that specific release.

Now, let's look at some practical tips that I found useful.

Practical tips on prioritizing requirements

Let us look at a few pointers that might help you with your prioritization activities. They are very useful and important and can potentially save you a lot of pain and time. Some practical tips that you may find useful during your project implementations are:

- Ensure that every team member on the project and all your stakeholders understand the flow of the process.

- Refrain from automating everything in the initial releases. Focus on the core functionality that will add more functions to the system even though they require more steps from users.

- Understand the usage and feedback from users for steps that you plan to automate. Does it really make sense to automate these steps? Do your business users want that automated, or are they comfortable with the way it is?

- Avoid automating edge cases. If this feature is used rarely or by only a small set of users, do you really want to automate these steps? To mitigate any risk in these situations, you can generate a simple email notification to your sales operations/planning team to verify these edge cases.

- Create a roadmap for automation when you have a multi-release project. This will help with negotiating trade-offs between automation versus adding new features/functions.

- Manage expectations by progressive prioritization and by being transparent. Let all your stakeholders and project team members have access to your **business requirements document (BRD)** or product backlog.

- Set expectations of stakeholders that not all requirements may be implemented. Have a rollout roadmap published and communicated.

- Ask the right question:

  - What problem are we trying to solve?

  - What happens if we implement it?

  - What happens if we do not implement it?

- Involve the right stakeholder who is relevant to a specific session. Involve users directly and indirectly impacted by the functionality your project plans to implement.

- Not all stakeholders are the same. Some have a bigger say on what to prioritize because of their rank, knowledge, role, and so on. Be cognizant of this, and if it is simple to do, it is advisable to deliver low-hanging fruits and earn these influential stakeholders' trust.

- Whenever you re-prioritize, make sure you are not breaking some other functionality. Always check for dependencies between requirements and technology capabilities.

- Some requirements have to be prioritized as high because they may differentiate your product compared to other competitor products for political reasons (such as you want to release the feature for a major conference) and improve adoption/usability (if adoption and usability are already an issue).

- Prioritizing high-risk requirements early will help you mitigate the risk and find alternative options in the event it does not work out.

- You have to implement some requirements that may have a lower priority. We create a **minimum viable product** (MVP) and implement only the core functionality with minimal effort, which can be enhanced later. This effort will help you gain their trust and create excitement and interest. Do it wisely. Your main opposition will be your project manager.

- Start prioritizing efforts early. Start tagging them as High, Medium, or Low. Keep reviewing them iteratively and keep the document current. Priorities change as the requirements age.

Ensuring all team members understand the functional and non-functional requirements and process flows and then getting consensus and common agreement are the most difficult tasks for project team members. If enough time is dedicated to doing this task, this will lay the foundation for the success of your project. Now, let's summarize this chapter.

Summary

In this chapter, we checked all the automation features that are available in Salesforce. You now know the benefits of automating steps in a phased manner to add real value to your business users. We saw the benefit of creating and communicating an automation roadmap and finally concluded with a few tips and tricks.

With this, we conclude *Part 1* of the book, and you can understand what functional requirements are and how process flow ties into functional requirements. Also, we discussed how every team member's understanding of process flow can help you decide what to and what not to automate. In the next part, we will get into Salesforce flows.

You are now well positioned to do the following:

- Identify the right set of requirements that can be automated

- Understand business needs and hence able to solution design what to and what not to automate

- Avoid too much automation due to a lack of planning

- Now assess the impact of existing and planned automation resulting in automation logic executing randomly

In the next part, you will learn how to automate your business processes using Salesforce flows. Flows provide wonderful functionality where you will be able to declaratively and, to some extent, using minimal coding knowledge, implement your business processes by automating them using this flow feature. This part will help you learn tools, techniques, and methods you can implement and incorporate to transform business needs into working automated functions in your system.

In the next chapter, we will dive into understanding the main building block of Salesforce flows, ways to trigger flows and entry/exit conditions of flows.

Questions

1. What are some proven process model examples?
2. Which tools can you use to create process models?
3. Name a few ways to automate business process steps in Salesforce.

Further reading

- *Scheer, August-Wilhelm, Saarbrucken, Henrik von Scheel, Mark von Rosing (2014). The Complete Business Process Handbook: Body of Knowledge from Process Modeling to BPM, Volume 1. Morgan Kaufmann Publishers Inc.*

- *Business process (Wikipedia):* https://en.wikipedia.org/wiki/Business_process

- *Srini Munagavalasa (2022). The Salesforce Business Analyst Handbook, Part 1. Packt Publishing Ltd.*

Part 2: Business Process Automation in Salesforce

In this part, you will learn the next phase of the automation cycle – how to automate your business processes using Salesforce Flows. Flows provide a wonderful functionality where you shall be able to declaratively and to some extent minimal coding knowledge and implement your business processes by automating them using this flow feature. This part will help you learn tools, techniques, and methods you can implement and incorporate to transform business needs into working automated functions in your system.

In this part, we'll discuss some of the challenges that we face in most Salesforce projects, and suggest methods to handle them:

- Admins and business analysts often overlook Salesforce Flows due to their perception as a tool intended for only advanced technical team members.

- Implementing an automated feature as requests come in from end users.

- Team members do not understand the flow execution order and do not implement the right flow technique.

- Lack of awareness around screen flows to help end users guide through business processes via user input.

The following chapters will be covered in this part.

- *Chapter 4, Flow Building Blocks, Triggering, and Entry Conditions*

- *Chapter 5, Salesforce Order of Execution*

- *Chapter 6, Types of Salesforce Flows*

- *Chapter 7, Flows Using Apex Sharing*

- *Chapter 8, Optimizing and Troubleshooting Flows*

4

Flow Building Blocks, Triggering, and Entry Conditions

In this chapter, we will cover the main building blocks of Salesforce flows used in Flow Builder – **elements**, **connectors**, and **resources**. Then, we will discuss ways to trigger flow and entry/exit conditions. In this book, flows will be our primary tool where we will automate most tasks declaratively, such as workflows, email trigger notifications, field updates, and so on. The goal of this book is to explore and discuss automation tasks that can be performed with no-code and low-code users such as your system admins or business analysts. You will be able to understand the concepts of Salesforce flows and get equipped to start creating a flow at your organization.

We will cover the following topics in this chapter:

- Flow building blocks
- Flows to trigger business processes
- Flow entry and exit conditions
- Key considerations

By the end of this chapter, you will understand the previously mentioned three main building blocks of flows, how to trigger them, and entry and exit conditions.

A valid requirement may evolve into an invalid requirement at a future date based on factors such as changes in business processes, operating environmental factors, changes in stakeholders, and so on.

Flow building blocks

Before we get into flow building blocks, let's take a step back and define flows and a tool to build flows called **Flow Builder**.

Salesforce flows are a visual algorithm of your process flow. They are based on flowchart models – these are a visual representation of the process in a sequence of steps and decision points. While process flows are depicted using flowcharts and are static, Salesforce flows are dynamic and living flowcharts that we can use to implement our business processes. Flow Builder is our tool that makes these flows come to life. The best part is that they are declarative automation features that team members can implement with low code.

Flow Builder utilizes all these building blocks and helps us create these flows on a canvas. Let's take a look and learn the flow of building blocks.

There are three building blocks that we need for any Salesforce flow. They are as follows:

- **Elements**: This is a step that tells the flow what to do. There are many elements that can do different things. There are three types of elements:

  - **Interaction element**: User interaction is needed to trigger this flow element. These are screen elements where the user can interact with data on the screen, and action elements make the interaction feasible.

  - **Data element**: Provides instruction to interact with database records or records. We use data elements to read, create, update, and delete records.

  - **Logic element**: Enables flow to evaluate and manipulate data as per your business process flows (requirements). It helps us decide what we would like to do with the data, such as define criteria for multiple paths, pause flows, create looping paths, and so on.

  From the toolbar, as shown in *Figure 4.1*, we will be able to create these elements by dragging and dropping them on the canvas. We will explore the canvas in detail and create multiple flow scenarios in the coming chapters:

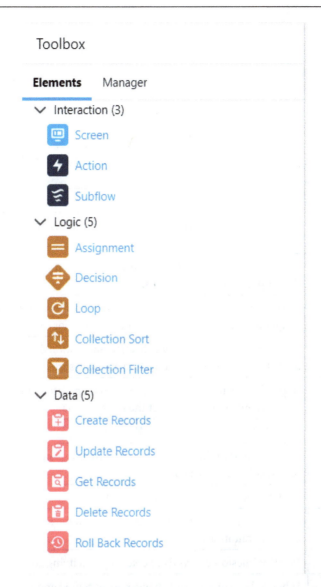

Figure 4.1 – Flow elements as represented on Salesforce Flow Builder

You can find high-level definitions of each element in *Figure 4.2*:

Elements	
Interaction (3)	
Screen	The screen lets you capture or display information to a user.
Action	Call an Apex class and perform an action.
Subflow	Launch another active flow within the organization. Also called a referenced flow.
Logic (5)	
Assignment	Used to set values – variables, collection variables, record variables, record collection variables, and global variables.
Decision	Based on a set of conditions, and routes users through the flow based on the output of those conditions.
Loop	A loop path for iterating over items in a collection variable. The flow temporarily stores the item in the loop variable for each iteration of the loop.
Collection Sort	Reorder the items within a collection and optionally limit the number of items that remain in the collection after the sort.
Collection Filter	Apply filter criteria to a collection, and then output a new collection that contains only items that meet the filter criteria.
Data (5)	
Create Records	Create one or multiple Salesforce records by using a record variable or a record collection variable.
Update Records	Update one or more Salesforce records.
Get Records	Find Salesforce records and store values from the records in variables based on filter conditions.
Delete Records	Identify Salesforce records to delete by specifying conditions.
Roll Back Records	When a flow runs, record changes are executed and saved to the database as part of a transaction. This element rolls back the current transaction and cancels all its pending record changes.

Figure 4.2 – Flow element high-level definitions

- **Connectors**: These direct the flow to which element to execute next. Basically, they determine the flow path. They define the path that the flow takes from start to finish as it runs.

Various elements of a flow are connected via lines with arrows on the canvas. This is the path our flow runs when executed. For a simplified flow with connectors, see *Figure 4.3*. Each element should be connected via a connector to our screen flow so that the steps are performed in this sequence to create a contact record in Salesforce.

In free-form, you create and remove connectors that determine the order of execution for the elements on the canvas, whereas in auto-layout, Flow Builder automatically creates or removes connectors.

In our next screenshot, we can clearly see how the connectors are connected between different canvas elements. The **Get Records** element is connected to the decision element. The **Decision** element is connected to the **Create Records** data element. The direction of the connector arrow gives us the direction in which the flow gets executed:

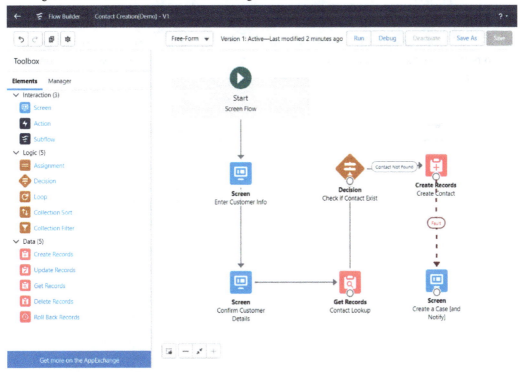

Figure 4.3 – Contact Creation Flow Builder layout; elements are connected via connectors

You can navigate to the **Flow Builder** page from **Setup | Flow** and then click on one of your flows (or one of the **Managed-Installed** flows provided by Salesforce; for example, **Create a Case**).

- **Resources**: Resources are individual variables that we use in Flow Builder to create flows. They can be text, numbers, records, text templates, variables, picklist values, and so on. Some resources, such as global constants and global variables, are provided by the system. You do not see them on the canvas, but they are referenced by the flow's elements. To see all your resources, click on the **Manager** tab on your Flow Builder. We can access them while editing the elements. These containers store values to enable specific business functions related to the flow. They are useful only when the flow is running.

A resource can be any of the following:

- A value
- A global resource
- Fields
- Records
- Multiple records
- Elements

See *Figure 4.4*. The value for **Field** is stored in the variables, and these variables are our resources to hold values during the flow execution. You can view this screen by double-clicking on one of the data elements such as **Get Records**:

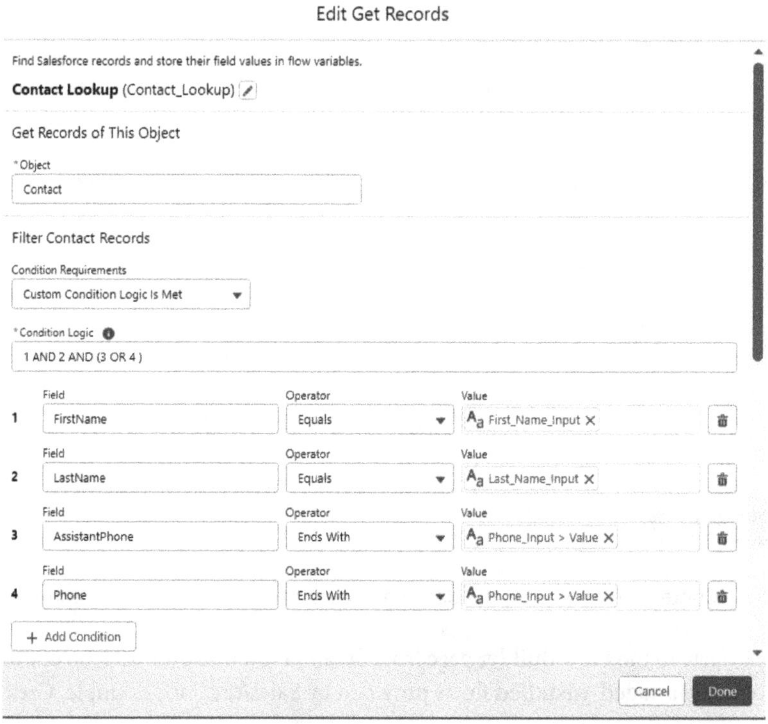

Figure 4.4 – Get Records element in edit mode; here, we can assign resources to our fields

- The `First_Name_Input` (`{!First_Name_Input}`) resource is a variable that holds a value for **FirstName**

- The `Last_Name_Input` `{!Last_Name_Input}` is a variable that holds a value for **LastName**

These resource values are available only during the running of our flow. Once the flow ends, these values are purged, and resources are ready for a new set of values.

Now that we have gained an understanding of the basic building blocks of flows, the next section lets us learn various flows that we have in Salesforce that trigger your business steps and hence automate your business process.

Flows to trigger business processes

We have seen various building blocks – elements, connectors, and resources. We use these basic building blocks to enable and trigger our business process steps. Based on the business process requirements, processes can be interactive with your end users, or they can run behind the scenes seamlessly.

There are two ways flows can be triggered:

1. **Interactive experience flows**: Here, users need to input or perform interactively on the screen. A good example would be to collect customer information and contact information on one simple **user interface (UI)** and let the flow take care of updates to multiple objects.

2. **Behind-the-scenes automated flows**: No user action is required. These flows run behind the scenes, and we can say they are 100% automated. *Example*: Generate an email notification to the account manager when a high-value opportunity status is changed to **Closed Lost**. Another example would be scheduling notifications for all open opportunities to the sales manager, a week before the opportunity close date.

Let's take an in-depth look at these two ways with some examples.

Interactive experience flows

There are five ways we can interact with the screen to trigger the flow. They are as follows:

1. **Screen flows**: This can be triggered via user interactions such as screens, actions, and so on.

2. **Autolaunched flows**: Autolaunched flows can be triggered by user interaction to launch this flow; for example, by clicking a custom button on the screen or another flow (subflow), or API calls from an external system.

3. **Approval processes**: Approval processes let us specify a sequence of steps that are required with assigned approvers to approve a record. *Example*: Quote with a large amount requiring three levels of approvals based on the Product family.

4. **Visualforce pages**: Used to build highly interactive and complex screens using HTML and Apex code.

5. **Lightning components**: As with Visualforce pages, these use HTML and JavaScript code.

Behind-the-scenes automated flows

There are four behind-the-scenes flows available:

1. **Record-triggered flows**: These are triggered when a record is created, updated, or deleted, and they run in the background. *Example*: Creating records and sending emails to owner and account team members.

2. **Scheduled-triggered flows**: These can be triggered via a schedule at a scheduled time and frequency such as daily background jobs, notifications, and so on.

3. **Platform event-triggered flows**: These flows are triggered based on system event messages.

4. **Apex flows**: Reusable block of automation code that can be triggered in the background. *Example*: Say we need to remove access to an opportunity if it is marked confidential, such as **MNPI** (short for **material non-public information**), or private. In these situations, an Apex block of code removes team members on **Account and Opportunities**.

Now that we have learned about flow building blocks and how to trigger these flows, let us quickly review what entry and exit conditions are.

Flow entry and exit conditions

We have our building blocks and our flows to trigger a business process flow, so let's now explore and see when they should be triggered and when they should exit. Just like how we develop business process flows, we need a process start and a process end. The entry conditions will trigger our flow. *Example*: When the opportunity stage changes to stage 50%, create a quote with product line items and assign a task to a sales team member.

Here, the change in opportunity stage is our entry condition, and assigning a task will be our exit condition. In case the flow fails, we need an exception message to the technical team, and in this case, this exception message will be an exit condition.

Entry conditions in Salesforce flows can be triggered by the following:

*   **Screen flows**: Users can trigger via interactions on the screen. The entry criteria here is user input data on the screen that triggers the flow and exit with DML operations such as insert or update.

*   **Scheduled flows**: We can have a flow triggered on a specific date and/or at a specific time. Here, the entry criteria are obviously date/time. What if it fails? In this case, make sure you capture the exception and notify your admin or your sales ops team.

- **Record changes**: Updating a record can trigger a case, task, email, and so on. An example of this scenario would be an update to opportunity stages with a high probability of winning, generating a draft contract in Salesforce or another part system.

- **Platform events**: Platform events such as create, update, delete, and so on can trigger flows. Here, a start condition is an action on the record such as insert, update, and so on.

- **Autolaunched flows**: These are triggered via the **Custom** button, another flow, and other automation (Apex code, Visualforce page). One example would be a user clicking on the **Custom** button on demand to launch the flow and send a quote to your contract team.

Exit conditions in Salesforce flows can be triggered by the following:

- **Exit flows**: Every process should have an exit condition that terminates the flow. This can be done by displaying a message, sending a notification, or updating the customer flag based on the type of flow:

  - Iterative logic such as loops should have exit conditions well defined. If not, the loops run iteratively, draining resources.

- **Error message/notification**: In case of a failed flow, every flow should have an error-capturing and -notification mechanism:

  - To ensure this DML operation went successfully, send an email message notifying the users. In case of failure, make sure you catch this exception via an error message to the user or your admin.

  - In case of failure, another good exit criterion would be to post to Chatter or create a case.

Entry conditions are obvious but exit conditions are not. What happens in the case of exceptions? How do you know if certain actions such as database updates triggered via flow automations are successful? The best way to find this out is to send some kind of notification or Chatter post, and so on. These conditions will be discussed in the future chapters in detail.

In this section, I would like to emphasize that planning entry and exit conditions is particularly important for making your flows complete so that your business can confidently rely on them. You may be wondering why this additional work needs to be done when we do various rounds of testing to ensure our development works as designed. Well, testing cannot cover every scenario, plus test results are valid at that point in time. At a future date, additional functionality may be added, and that may disrupt our existing functionality. It is always good to get confirmation that what is planned got delivered as planned. Think of this as a delivery confirmation message that you receive when what you ordered is delivered. It will be even better if you can add product details such as high-level details and link these to records so that users can easily navigate to the records. (Think of how Amazon adds a picture of your product when it is delivered to your front door.)

Key considerations

Before you even venture into flows, make sure you take these key items into consideration:

- You and the project team need to be conversant with process flows, especially the "to-be" future state flow.

- To be able to define entry criteria and flow triggers, understand the persona, such as who will run the flow, which steps need to be executed, and when.

- Always consider exit criteria too. This is very important and needs to be accounted for. What do you want the flow to do if a step fails? How do we confirm that a given step in the flow is executed successfully?

- Plan out the complete flow visually on a flip chart or white paper and run it by a few SMEs. This will help you consolidate your understanding as well as make it easier when you create the flow in your Salesforce system.

- To do data loads, consider building a bypass in your flows to avoid hitting governor limits.

- Check and see if you are looping over large data volumes that could trigger the flow element limit.

- Do not use DML elements inside of a loop in an autolaunched flow or record-triggered flow. If you have to, use the new In/Not in operators.

With these few key considerations, let's summarize this chapter before moving on to the next chapter.

Summary

In this chapter, we understood what flows are made up of, various triggering mechanisms, and their entry/exit criteria, which will help you design and develop successful Salesforce flows that effectively confirm your business process flows and meet your business needs. For this, you need a deep understanding of your business process flow, and then, for each step of the flow, check for the following aspects:

- What are the flow building blocks can I use?

- How do I plan to trigger that business process step?

- What are your entry (input) and exit (output) criteria?

In the next chapter, we will explore and see the **Order Of Execution** (**OOE**) of how your system runs various tasks in the backend. OOE was critical in general for technical teams in the past, but now it is more important for every Salesforce team member to understand it as flows are declarative and low code and can be created by your admins or business analysts.

Questions

1. How are autolaunched flows triggered?

2. What is the difference between autolaunched flows versus autolaunched flows (no trigger)?

3. Can you call any custom button from screen flows?

4. What is the major difference between **Actions** and **Custom** buttons?

Further reading

Flow Builder Basics: https://trailhead.salesforce.com/content/learn/modules/ flow-basics?trail_id=build-flows-with-flow-builder

Salesforce Order of Execution

In this chapter, we will explore the **Order Of Execution** (**OOE**) of how your system runs various tasks in the backend. OOE was critical in general only for technical teams in the past, but now it is more important for every Salesforce team member. As you know, flows are declarative and low-code and can be created by non-techies. Understanding the OOE with real-world examples will help you get comfortable, and this chapter will explore the concepts of execution by understanding how existing functionality will interact and affect new functionality and vice versa so as not to cause any technical debt.

In this chapter, we will cover the following sections to get a good grasp of Salesforce OOE:

- What is OOE?
- Salesforce Platform OOE
- Avoiding flow execution anti-patterns

Let us look at each of these in more detail.

What is OOE?

The OOE is a set of rules that describe the path your record takes through all available automation for a given object and all the events that happen from the user saving the record until the record is committed to the database.

When multiple automations such as workflows, assignment rules, escalation rules, roll-up summaries, and triggers are in place, it is crucial to know the sequence in which Salesforce processes these automations. The logical order in which the system processes these automation steps is termed the OOE.

We use software systems that help us create, read, update, and delete data many times a day. We all utilize SQL statements unknowingly every day, whether we're hardcore developers, system administrators, or even business team members. A good example would be your reports. You select fields from an object, filter the data, group it, limit it, and so on. How do we ensure that we get accurate data in our queries when we run our reports? Through the query execution plan, or the OOE of your SQL query.

System designers utilize this order to optimize database queries and minimize system resource usage. Understanding the OOE plan can help us optimize our queries and achieve better performance.

Do you know the OOE of our friendly `SELECT` statement? Your technical team will obviously know these concepts, but how about Salesforce administrators (and other not-so-technical team members)? As a non-technical team member, I may be tempted to think that `SELECT` statements are executed first. Think again.

Let us look at a simple `SELECT` statement that we often use to retrieve data from any system that uses a **DBMS** (short for **database management system**). We would like to display certain fields from database objects with filter criteria and summarize them in the desired order.

A sample Salesforce report to help jog your memory is shown next. This is a matrix report displaying all opportunities for the current fiscal year, grouped, aggregated, and sorted by region and country:

Sample-Opportunity Count by Region (FY2023 till date)

Region	Country	Prospecting Count	Qualification Count	Proposal Count	Negotiation Count	Closed Won Count	Closed Lost Count	Total Count
Americas	Brazil	53	16	13	19	41	20	162
	Canada	26	23	10	33	61	3	156
	Chile	17	25	10	0	25	5	82
	Colombia	10	0	2	0	3	1	16
	Mexico	5	7	4	4	4	9	33
	US	71	36	25	27	110	30	299
APAC	Hong Kong	79	88	19	34	140	13	373
	India	59	32	11	22	37	5	166
	Indonesia	25	30	16	15	46	1	133
	Malaysia	30	16	5	9	19	4	83
	Philippines	48	32	2	20	14	2	118
	Singapore	110	50	20	21	50	25	276
EMEA	England	56	69	29	22	28	10	214
	France	39	24	5	25	30	7	130
	Germany	15	10	10	7	10	5	57
	Italy	10	11	10	6	18	5	60
	Total	653	469	191	264	636	145	2358

Report Date - 12/31/2023

Figure 5.1 – Sample-Opportunity Count by Region report

To get accurate output from your reports, you must ensure that your query executes as intended. For this reason, by understanding the OOE, you will be in a better position to effectively and quickly design and create reports. The preceding opportunity report used an SQL statement.

This is a typical SQL statement, and one would think it gets executed in the order it is laid out here:

```
SELECT <select list>
    FROM <object source>
    WHERE <search condition>
    GROUP BY <group by expression>
    HAVING <search condition>
    ORDER BY <order expression>
```

SQL is a declarative language, not a procedural language. The SQL compiler and optimizer determine which operations are actually run. The SQL engine will execute the clauses in a specific, predetermined order called the OOE. Understanding the OOE helps us to write better queries as well as troubleshoot issues faster.

This is the typical logical order of SQL statement execution, with exceptions in uncommon cases:

1. The FROM clause retrieves data from the table(s).
2. JOIN subclauses specify rules for joining tables.
3. The WHERE clause includes a comparison predicate, which helps restrict the rows returned by the query.
4. The GROUP BY clause projects rows with common values into a smaller set of rows.
5. The HAVING clause is used to filter rows resulting from the GROUP BY clause.
6. SELECT will retrieve data from one or more tables.
7. The DISTINCT keyword eliminates duplicate data.
8. The ORDER BY clause identifies columns to use to sort the resulting data and sort direction.

This is also called **binding order**, which means what is defined in a given step is available in subsequent steps to the query processor. Similarly, anything defined in later steps is not available in prior steps. *Example*: An object defined in the FROM clause can be accessed from any step, whereas column aliases defined in the SELECT step cannot be used in prior steps such as the WHERE clause or the GROUP BY clause.

> **Note**
>
> To get more details on SQL OOE, check out these links:
>
> - Logical processing order of the SELECT statement (*Microsoft Learn - SELECT (Transact-SQL)*): https://learn.microsoft.com/en-us/sql/t-sql/queries/select-transact-sql?view=sql-server-ver16
> - *Secret to Optimizing SQL Queries*: https://youtu.be/BHwzDmr6d7s?si=vrjeoPGOto85LmSs

Now, I guess you understand why OOE is so critical. Getting a good grasp and understanding of these concepts will help you better plan and implement Salesforce flows in your organization.

With this understanding, let's take a look at OOE in Salesforce in the next section.

Salesforce Platform OOE

As with every other software application, Salesforce also defines its own set of OOE in its database. Without these rules and controls in place, we will run into unexpected behaviors in our data as well as the overall behavior and performance of the system, not to mention implications for your organization.

This is OOE as defined by Salesforce. No matter what kind of tool you use, this order needs to be followed. It can be your Apex coding, Salesforce flows, or something else.

This is the sequence in which Salesforce executes various tasks. When any DML operation is performed in a Salesforce record, such as your user clicking the **Save** button to create or update a record, the following is the OOE in Salesforce:

1. Initializes the record (the original record loaded from the database for updates).

2. **System validation rules**: Loads new values (for updates, old values are replaced). This event verifies field formats, maximum field lengths, required fields at the layout level, and so on.

3. Executes before-save record-triggered flows. This is used for operations on records that triggered the flow, such as updating the record fields with the next values.

4. Executes all before Apex triggers.

5. Runs most system validation and custom validation rules.

6. Executes duplicate rules if you have duplicate rules defined in your system.

7. **Saves the record to the database (no commit to the database)**: This is to ensure that the saved data rolls back in the event of issues downstream. Record ID and system fields are available on soft save.

8. Executes all after Apex triggers.

9. **Executes assignment rules**: All your lead or case assignment rules get executed here. If you have an after-save record trigger flow updating a lead or case object, assignment rule values will be overwritten due to the OOE.

10. **Executes auto-response rules**: Any auto-lead or case-auto-response rules get executed here.

11. **Executes workflow rules**: This runs only when a field is updated. Even though this feature is no longer available to create new workflow rules, you may have old workflows pending migration to flows.

12. **Executes escalation rules**: Any case-time-dependent case escalations or service escalations rules get triggered here.

13. Executes Salesforce Flow automation:

    • We have the option to specify a trigger order value, and it is available for before-save or after-save flows by object

    • Flows with the same trigger with values from 1 to 1,000 run in ascending order

- Flows with the same trigger order value run in alphabetical order based on the flows' API names

- Flows that are unordered run next based on created dates

- Flows with a trigger order from 1,001 to 2,000 run next and in ascending order

14. Executes after-save record-triggered flows. This operation is used for updating related records.

15. Executes entitlement rules, if any, to meet SLAs for your customers.

16. Updates to the roll-up summary field on parent records first after performing all calculations.

17. Updates to the roll-up summary field on grandparent records (if applicable).

18. **Executes a criteria-based sharing evaluation**: A sharing rule created with the rule type as criteria-based sharing to grant access to records is executed during this step.

19. **Commits all DML operations to the database**: This step ensures data is committed to the database.

20. After the changes are committed to the database, post-commit logic is executed, such as sending emails, asynchronous Apex jobs, future methods, and so on.

These steps are executed in order, and in many instances, we may see iterative loops of trigger executions, and then it continues down until the post-commit logic is executed. An example would be, say, an after-save trigger that creates a new record. This will start the loop from *step 1* for this new record, as it needs to go through all the steps. So, it starts with *step 1* and eventually ends at *step 20*, but within these steps, there may be many iterative loops based on the complexity of your triggers.

Now that you understand the basics of how Salesforce triggers OOE rules, let's quickly review some misconceptions that may derail our flow-building process. Reviewing them now during the early phases will help the project team identify and fix them during the development phase. Let us see which flow execution anti-patterns we need to pay attention to.

> **Note**
>
> All actions performed before the *Saves the record to the database (no commit to the database)* step (*step 7*) after generating the record ID can be considered a before-save event, and any action occurring after this is an after-save trigger.

Avoiding flow execution anti-patterns

You may be wondering why this topic is discussed now and not at the end of the book. Here, I would like to emphasize that we need to plan for this right from the early phases of the project, even before any development of flows is started. You, as a builder of flows, need to understand this conceptually with reference to the business process flow. Make a note on your business process flow diagram (similar to the one in *Figure 3.1*) so that you can revisit it as the project progresses. We will revisit the same topic in *Part 3* of this book.

Just because you would like to implement a cool tool (in this case, our all-powerful Flow Builder) does not necessarily mean you should use flows for everything. It may not always make sense to implement flows all the time. Let's look at some anti-patterns that we tend to implement. Think through it and do some exploratory analysis before you jump to conclusions.

Screen flows are good to have for your users if they help them do something quickly and effectively. But if they are cluttered with many fields and if they mandate different users to have different access at the field level, think of using a page layout. With record types and page layout combinations, you are more likely to have better success than with Salesforce flows.

Do not start working on the flow builder without having agreed and approved business process flow diagrams. The person who is responsible for creating flows should understand each and every aspect of the process flow steps. Business process flow diagrams, for the most part, take you through the path of success (also called the *happy path*). This means the business process moves from start to finish nicely and smoothly. Well, that is exactly what our business needs. When you come to flows in Salesforce, you need go a few steps ahead and think "What if?" at each step of the process. What if it fails? Do we have an exception handler for fault paths? How do we address this failure? Make a note of the business process flow chart and what you plan to address.

If your business processes are simple, then you may not need to worry too much about planning them, but this is rare for most of our implementations. For medium and complex implementations with a large volume of users, I have seen business process flows get extremely complex. What we do in this situation is take chunks of functionality as different business process flows and refer the main flow to this smaller independent flow. This way, it will be more manageable to maintain the flow as well as for the team members to understand. This is exactly what you need to do with Salesforce flows. Use sub-flows and make your complex flow more readable; we will explore this in *Chapter 10*.

Do you have complex logic and large volumes of data to be processed as part of business logic? Salesforce flows can do looping and handle multiple records, but there is **technical debt**. How, you may ask? Just because Flow Builder is a point-and-click tool doesn't mean there is no code involved. Under the hood, Salesforce did all this complex coding for you. If you plan to process large amounts of records as part of flow triggers, think again and do your due diligence. For example, when you hit governor limits and flow limits, check and see if you are looping over large data volumes that could trigger the flow element limit. If you have to use DML elements inside a loop in a flow, what is the best course of action? Do you often do high-volume data loads, and did you consider building bypasses in your flows? Maybe your technical team members can do a better and more effective job via Apex triggers.

If your business process is relatively complex, take the help of your technical architect and developers in designing and developing Salesforce flows. To design and create complex flows, you need some level of understanding of Apex code. If you are confident that you can do it, go ahead, but get it reviewed by your solution architect or one of your technical team members.

Finally, just because it says it is point-and-click does not mean you can skip some levels of testing. Plan for various testing cycles such as SIT, regression, UAT, and so on, just like you test the rest of the functionality. Putting effort into testing will help identify and address edge cases and exceptions.

We can keep going on and on. My point here is to inform you to keep an eye out, take notes, and verify and validate your findings and understanding as you progress so that you can deliver exceptional flows that don't just work but work effectively.

Summary

In this chapter, we reviewed why OOE is not only important but also critical for designing and developing flow to meet your business needs. We also reviewed a few anti-patterns that you should keep an eye on and think about while designing, developing, and testing your flows.

Remember to consider the OOE for all automation done inside and outside your flows. If you have an Apex trigger and a flow on the same given object at the same time, you need to understand in which order these are executed.

In the next chapter, we will explore five basic types of flows to automate our business processes. You will gain a deep understanding of the scenarios for each of the flow types: screen flows, record trigger flows, schedule trigger flows, platform event-triggered flows, and autolaunched flows.

Questions

1. We have a case assignment rule before saving a record-triggered flow, and it happens both times to update the case owner. Who wins? The case assignment rule or the before-save record-triggered flow?

2. Do you have control over when a specific flow during the execution of Salesforce flow automation can run?

3. Why do we need to understand Salesforce OOE?

4. What happens when a roll-up summary field on parents gets updated? What happened to the OOE for this parent record?

Further reading

- *Part 1* of *The Salesforce Business Analyst Handbook*

- *Salesforce Platform-Order-Of-Execution-Diagram*: https://architect.salesforce.com/1/asset/immutable/s/e6cf2ac/assets/images/Salesforce-Order-Of-Execution-Diagram.png

- *Apex Developer Guide - Triggers and Order of Execution*: https://developer.salesforce.com/docs/atlas.en-us.apexcode.meta/apexcode/apex_triggers_order_of_execution.htm

- *Salesforce Ben-Learn Salesforce Order of Execution*: https://www.salesforceben.com/learn-salesforce-order-of-execution/

- *Guidelines for Defining the Run Order of Record-Triggered Flows for an Object* (salesforce.com): https://help.salesforce.com/s/articleView?id=sf.flow_concepts_trigger_guidelines.htm&type=5

- *Select (SQL)*: https://en.wikipedia.org/wiki/Select_(SQL)

6

Types of Salesforce Flows

This chapter will explore the five basic types of flows to automate our business processes. You will gain a deep understanding of scenarios for each of the flow types – screen flows, record-triggered flows, schedule-triggered flows, platform event-triggered flows, and autolaunched flows. We can create flows that let users interact with a user interface, initiated by screen flow, and run them automatically based on **Data Manipulation Language** (**DML**) actions. We will explore scheduled flows that can be scheduled at a future time and frequency, as well as platform event triggers that are triggered based on platform event messages.

We will cover the following Salesforce flow sections:

- The five basic types of flows in Salesforce:

  - Exploring screen flows

  - Exploring record-triggered flows

  - Exploring schedule-trigger flows

  - Exploring platform event-triggered flows

  - Exploring autolaunched flows

- Practical tips for success

We will review each of these automation flow types in detail, with practical examples, and explore the type of flow that makes sense to automate your business processes. You will learn each flow and its concept so that you can make an informed decision when you start planning your business process automation in Salesforce using Flow Builder. You rarely resort to just one flow type. Your business is complex, and so are your business processes, so to simplify these complex scenarios for your users, you will resort to more than one flow type. These complex scenarios will be covered in *Part 3* of the book when we explore the flow orchestration tool. For now, in this chapter, let's focus on each individual flow type, one at a time, and try to grasp the concepts.

Let us look at each of these in more detail.

Exploring five basic types of flows in Salesforce

In Salesforce, there are five basic (core) types of flows available via the Flow Builder tool. They are as follows:

- **Screen flow**: This guides users through a business process interactively and can be launched from lightning pages, custom buttons, actions, custom links, **Lightning Web Components** (**LWC**), and Experience Builder pages. An example of a screen flow is service agents collecting data from customers that can be used to update records, such as shipping addresses, or create cases.

- **Record-triggered flow**: This is triggered by DML actions such as record, create, update, or delete. An example of a record-triggered flow is when the opportunity stage is won, you close all quotes related to the opportunity and notify the deal registration team.

- **Schedule-triggered flow**: This launches at a specified time and frequency for each record in a batch. The autolaunched flow runs in the background and is triggered based on parameters and logic. An example of a schedule-triggered flow is one that runs every day at 1 a.m. to send a mass notification to the opportunity owner that a closing date has passed, reminding them to work on closing the opportunity.

- **Platform event-triggered flow**: This launches when a platform event message is received. This autolaunched flow runs in the background. These events can be internal or external to Salesforce. An example of a platform event-triggered flow is when an order is placed, using the Salesforce platform, and shipping notifications are sent to the delivery team.

- **Autolaunched flow** (**no trigger**): Here, a trigger is not defined within the flow. Autolaunched flows run in the background and are initiated by custom buttons and custom links, and they can be invoked by Apex, processes, REST API, and VF Pages. An example of an autolaunched flow is the sales operations team wanting to send an account business plan as a PDF document to the account manager and customer contacts.

Now, let's see how to access flows in Salesforce, take a look at the **New Flow** screen, and then get into exploring each flow type in detail.

Accessing flows in Salesforce

In this section, we will take a quick look at the Flow Builder and look at the landing page where we will be able to create the aforementioned five basic flows. To create flows, we use the **Flow Builder** user interface.

Flow Builder is a powerful tool for building flows in Salesforce to automate business processes. It is a declarative interface, and with clicks and low code, we can create code-like logic without actually coding. It has a toolbox with resources and elements that we can use to build a flow.

To navigate to Flows, go to **Setup (Platform Tools)** | **Process Automation** | **Flows**.

To view Flows in Salesforce, click on **New Flows** and **All + Templates**, as shown in *Figure 6.1*.

The **Core** tab will show you the basic flow, but the following view (**All + Templates**) will provide you with basic flows, as well as all the templates provided by Salesforce or third-party vendors via AppExchange. Explore various templates available out of the box, and see how they are developed. It's good practice to explore, understand, and repurpose these templates to cut down your development time.

Figure 6.1 - The five basic flow types

Now, let's go through each of these flow types with examples in detail. To create a specific flow type, select the flow and click on **Create**.

Screen flow

Screen flows help us enable functionality, where users are able to perform their business processes interactively via the Salesforce interface, which enables an excellent user experience. These screen flows can be enabled via quick actions or from lightning pages.

Here are the steps to create a screen flow:

1. Create a screen flow using the Flow Builder tool.
2. Add elements – data, logical, and screen elements – based on your requirements.
3. Add resources that you plan to use on the canvas, such as variables, screen components, and elements.
4. Connect these elements manually when using the free-form style on the canvas, whereas, in auto-layout, they are connected automatically as you add the elements to the screen layout. Play around, and pick the element that suits your taste.

5. Save and activate the flow. Before activation, debug the flow. We will discuss debugging in a later chapter.

6. Add this activated flow to a quick action or lightning page. This is where you launch your flow.

> **Note**
> You can have a screen flow accessible from every page by enabling the Lightning utility bar. This way, the Flow is available to users from every page. The utility bar is specific to a specific Lightning app, and it can be used to our advantage if we want to enable a screen flow for a specific group of users.

Now, let's look at a simplified practical scenario.

A business scenario for a screen flow

In this scenario, service agents will be able to capture shipping addresses from your customers from the **Account** page.

Let's capture this on a process flow from start to end. This is a simple scenario but very practical for easy understanding, although, in reality, Screen Flow can get very complex. Take notes as you draw this flow and while socializing with stakeholders.

The steps for this process are as follows:

1. The user clicks on a button or links on the screen (the page layout).

2. If the shipping address is the same as the billing address, copy the billing address to the shipping address (see the following note).

> **Note**
> You may be wondering why we need a screen flow to create a shipping address. Can't we directly add this address to the account record? Remember that your flows will be much more complex, and this is only a simple scenario. Also, with this flow, if you want to copy the billing address, all you need to do is select a checkbox.

3. If not, collect and input the shipping address.

4. Save the record and send a notification.

Before using your click and no-code skills in Salesforce, always create a process flow so that your team, including stakeholders, understands the business process flow conceptually (see *Figure 6.2*).

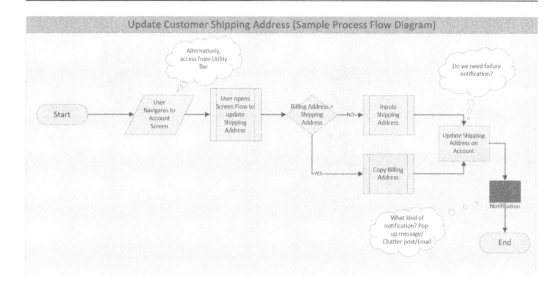

Figure 6.2 - Updating a customer shipping address (a process flow)

This process flow is easy to follow and self-explanatory. After the team agrees with the business process flow, you can create this in Salesforce using screen flows with simple clicks. When you start the flow say by clicking a button (or a link), the flow runs the screen element, and the flow remains on that element and waits for input. Based on the complexity of your business process, your flow might have multiple screens and, finally, a **Save** or **Cancel** button. After this final action, your screen flow ends.

The following steps are how I created this screen flow in Salesforce, also shown in *Figure 6.3* (use this in conjunction with *Figure 6.2* and follow along with the flow):

1. From Flow Builder, create a new screen flow.

2. Get billing address data from the account record – the user's **Get Records** data element.

3. Add a **Screen** element to capture the shipping address.

4. Add a **Decision** element to evaluate whether billing and shipping are the same.

5. Use two **Assignment** resources to assign, based on the decision in the prior step. If checked, copy the billing address to the variables; otherwise, keep the screen inputs.

6. Update the account record with the shipping address.

7. Add an **Action** element to notify address updates to users.

8. Optionally, for complex flow, we can add exception capture and notification mechanisms.

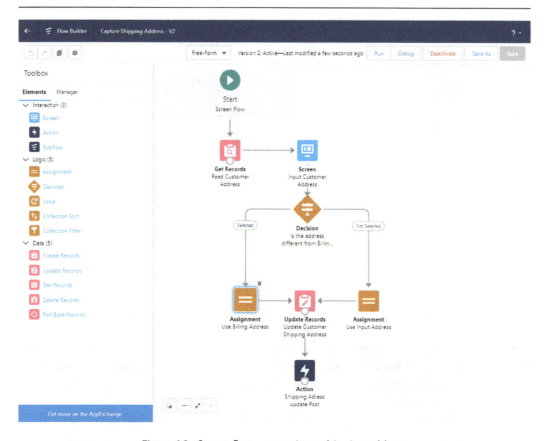

Figure 6.3 - Screen flow – capturing a shipping address

With simple clicks, your admins will be able to create a screen flow easily. Even though we focused on clicks and no-code, you still need to understand some level of technical details, such as our flow building blocks and resources. For you to be comfortable creating flows, you need to practice and understand how Salesforce flows work from a technical perspective (you also need to learn to debug them before you can promote them to your users in your production system). Learning any tool takes time, and Flow Builder is very easy to learn if you have good admin skills, BA skills, and lots of practice. Use Salesforce Trailhead and keep practicing. Check out *Screen Flows* at Salesforce Trailhead: `https://trailhead.salesforce.com/content/learn/modules/screen-flows?trail_id=build-flows-with-flow-builder`.

Let us see this screen flow trigger in execution.

In our scenario, it makes sense to add this to the Account Lightning page. The **Flow Action** button is created and also added to the Account Lightning page. As shown in *Figure 6.3*, if or when the user needs to create a shipping address, by clicking on this **Shipping Address(Flow)** button, they will be able to open the screen flow and input and save the data.

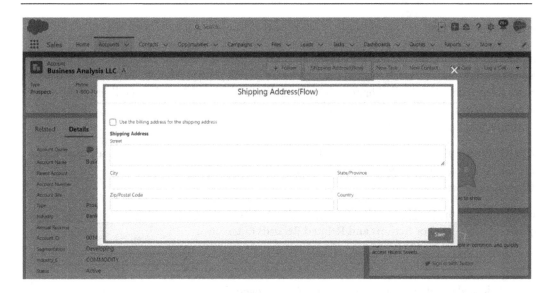

Figure 6.4 - A screen flow in action

Now that you have seen and have a good grasp of screen flows, you can see how easy it can be to create a flow with just a click. I recommend that you practice them a few times in the Trailhead playground. The best part is that the flows are visual. They are just like our business process flow. You can bring life to your business processes using Salesforce Flows. However, make sure to have your blueprint ready before you build your flow. This will help create effective and productive flows.

In the next section, let's explore the next flow type.

Record-triggered flow

Record-triggered flows allow us to automate actions based on Salesforce records that are created/updated/deleted. This action triggers our business processes behind the scenes. No user interaction is needed like with screen flows.

To create record-triggered Flows, we need to do the following:

1. Go to **Configure Start** (see *Figure 6.5*). This is the first step in creating a record-triggered flow. In this step, we select the object and entry criteria to trigger the flow.

2. Go to **Configure Scheduled Paths** (see *Figure 6.6*). This step is optional if we decide to run the flow immediately. This step helps us schedule a future time for the flow to run.

Configure Start

The starting point for this kind of flow is the object that triggers the flow. Then, we define when to trigger this flow. We can specify what DML operation should trigger this flow. Let's say, if someone deletes (record delete trigger) an opportunity, we, in the Sales department, can send a notification to the operations team queue. Alternatively, if the opportunity close date changed (record update trigger) to a future date, we could send a notification to the sales manager.

Next, we can add a condition. In our preceding example, the record is updated, and the opportunity close date is changed from one date to a future date. You can add multiple conditions, just as we do when we create Salesforce reports.

Finally, optimize the flow by deciding how and when you want to save the record – select **Fast Field Updates** (before-save) or **Actions and Related Records** (after-save).

> **Note**
>
> Fast field updates are similar to before-save Apex triggers. These are faster and recommended if you perform operations on the same record.
>
> Actions and related records are similar to after-save Apex triggers. We use these when we need to perform actions on related records or any after-save actions, such as creating tasks, sending emails, and Chatter posts.

In our example, since we need to operate the record, such as creating tasks or sending emails, we use an after-save trigger.

Let's see how we can create our record-triggered flow.

Go to **Setup** | **Process Automation** | **Flows** | **New Flow** | **Record-Triggered Flow** | **Create**. This will open the **Configure Start** screen, as shown in *Figure 6.5*.

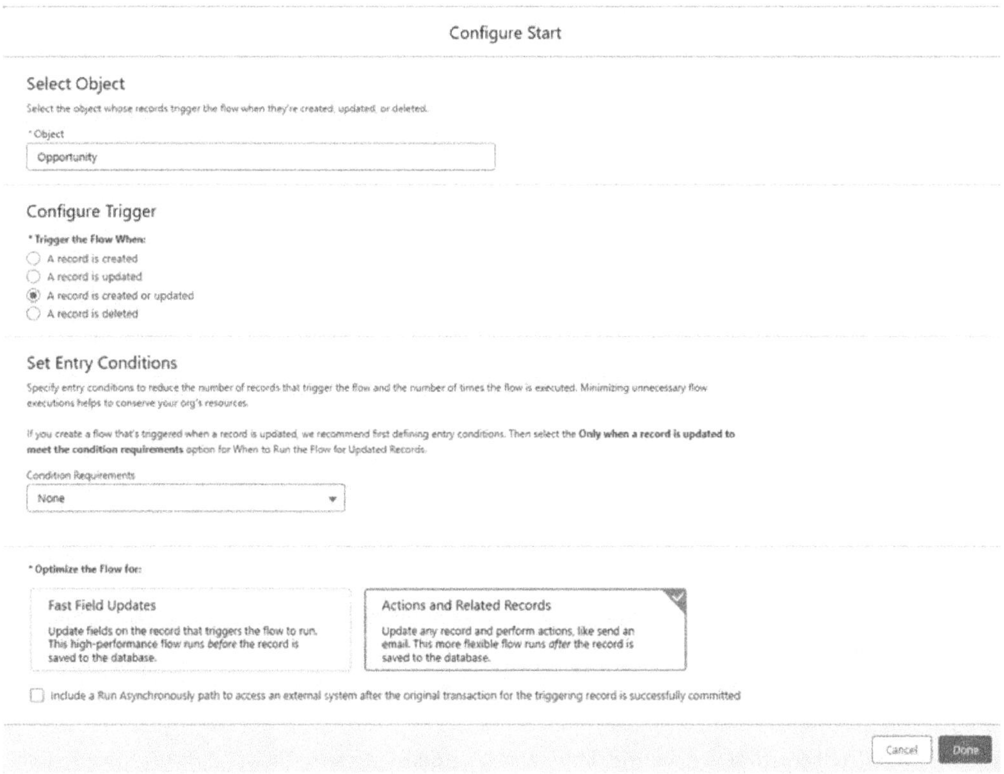

Figure 6.5 - A record-triggered flow – Configure Start

Configure Scheduled Paths

Next, we can define whether we would like to trigger this flow immediately and/or at specified dates. We can create multiple paths, as shown in *Figure 6.6*.

This step can be accessed from the record-triggered flow element on the canvas. Clicking on **Add Scheduled Paths (Optional)** will access the **Configure Scheduled Paths** screen. **Configure Scheduled Paths** is useful when we decide to run flows for a certain amount of time after the triggered record is created. The scheduled time can be for a triggered event, on a specified date, or a date and time in the record.

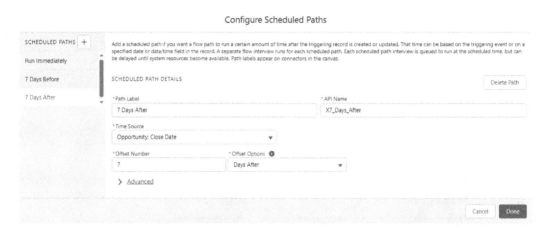

Figure 6.6 - A record-triggered flow – Configure Scheduled Paths

> **Note**
>
> When you create autolaunched flows, the **Screen** element is not available for us to add on the canvas. Autolaunched flows run in the background and user interaction is not needed, so we do not need a screen element.

To see our record-triggered flow in action, let us take a simple scenario.

A business scenario for a record-triggered flow

In this scenario, a sales analyst will get a reminder task created immediately and after three days of no activity on the opportunity, if 1) a high-value opportunity reaches a certain stage, or 2) the opportunity belongs to a premier customer. If there is no activity for seven days, escalation is sent to the account owner.

Let's see a record-triggered flow in action. To create it, we select the **Opportunity** object that triggers the flow, then we configure the trigger, set entry conditions with condition logic, and select the option to run the after-record save. In the following scenario, we create two tasks using **Create Records** elements and an escalation using the **Email Alert** action:

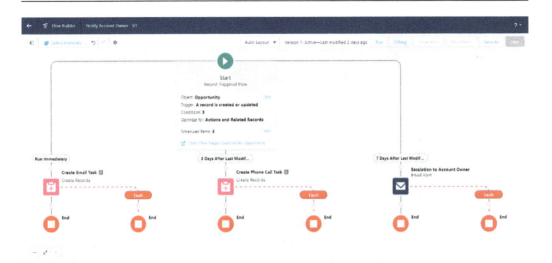

Figure 6.7 - A record-triggered flow – Notify Account Owner

- **Object**: In our scenario, we used the **Opportunity** object, whose records trigger the flow.

- **Conditions**: (1 AND 2) OR **3**: Amount is greater than $50,000 and the stage equals Negotiation/Review or customer type equals Premier:

  - Amount greater than or equal to $50,000

  - Stage = Negotiation/Review

  - Customer type = Premier

- **Actions and Related Records** (after-save): We pick this option as we are triggering action on other objects, such as creating tasks and a plan to send notifications in the future.

- **Scheduled Paths**: Our business scenarios state that we perform three actions – create a task immediately, another task three days after, and the last one seven days after:

  - **Run Immediately**
  - **3 Days After Last Modified Date**
  - **7 Days After Last Modified Date**

- Notification/Escalation:

  - Create Task – **Create Records** element: To create a task and assign this to Sales Analyst

  - Create Task – **Create Records** element: To create a task and assign this to the Sales Analyst (future-dated action)

  - Create Email Notification – **Email Alert**: To create an email alert for the account manager (a future-dated action)

- Exceptions – address failures:

  - Create **Fault** paths: Always create fault paths to catch exceptions

A record-triggered flow helps us automate common features such as notifications, creating tasks, and related records. They run automatically based on the status of the record, and if conditions are met, they trigger and do their job in the background. Always plan to capture exceptions and how to address them. In the preceding scenario, we have a fault path, and we would have posted on Chatter/send an email to admins so that we are aware of the issue firsthand.

In the next section, let's explore schedule-triggered flows.

A schedule-triggered flow

These flows launch based on a specified time and frequency, set by you for each record in a batch. When it is time, the autolaunched flow runs in the background.

To create a schedule-triggered flow, we start by setting a schedule.

These flows can be scheduled and run in the background from a scheduled start date, start time, and set frequency – once, daily, or weekly (see *Figure 6.8*).

You can access this page by clicking on **Add Scheduled Paths (Optional)** from the **Record-Triggered Flow** element on the canvas.

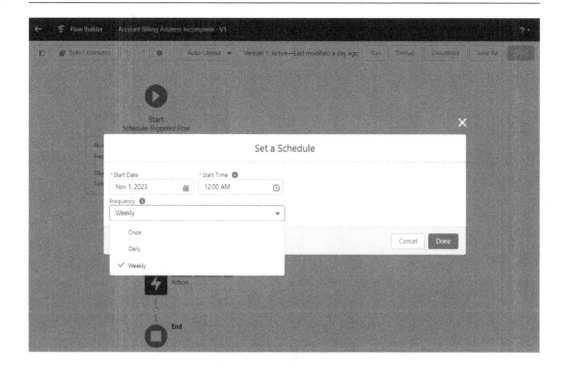

Figure 6.8 - A schedule-triggered flow – Account Billing Address Incomplete

After defining the schedule, we then specify the object and the conditions that each record must meet. Then, we update a flag on the object. Finally, we can post the data on Chatter or send an email notification to the team responsible for maintaining the quality of the data.

A simple scenario would be an incomplete billing address on account records causing many issues and delays in delivery, as well as an increase in customer complaints. This can be remediated very easily using a scheduled-triggered flow.

As shown in *Figure 6.9*, we create a flow to verify and check whether there are any missing fields – that is, incomplete billing addresses on our account records. If any of the fields are missing, we update an incomplete data flag on the account record and post it on Chatter (or send an email notification) so that our data quality team can address data issues.

Figure 6.9 - A schedule-triggered flow

Schedule-triggered flows can perform many of your automations in the background and can be scheduled during off hours when system resources are abundantly available. Now that you see how easy it is to create a schedule-triggered flow, try your hands at this flow type and add value to your business processes. In the next section, let's review platform event-triggered flows.

A platform event-triggered flow

A platform event is a special kind of Salesforce entity, just like a Salesforce object. An event message is an instance of a platform event, just like a record is an instance of a Salesforce object. Platform events allow event notifications to be sent back and forth between Salesforce and other systems. We can utilize platform events to create linkages between Salesforce business processes and other apps by exchanging real-time event data.

This flow runs when a platform event message is received. Platform events exchange real-time event data, and these events can be internal to Salesforce or can be from external systems. This autolaunched flow runs in the background and is triggered when a platform event message is received.

Let's look at a platform event trigger. In this scenario, we will capture errors in our screen flow execution. We use a standard Salesforce-provided platform event – a Flow Execution Error Event. This standard platform event notifies subscribers of any errors related to screen flow executions. Remember that it does not capture event notifications for other flow types.

A business scenario for a platform event trigger

This is a very simple scenario to understand and grasp concepts on how platform event triggers work. Our service agents capture customer contact information using a screen flow. Sometimes, the service agents forget to add the last name of the customer contact. Since the last name is mandated in our scenario, this flow fails. We will capture the flow error message and insert that into one of the custom objects.

Refer to more details on Flow Execution Error Events at `https://developer.salesforce.com/docs/atlas.en-us.platform_events.meta/platform_events/sforce_api_objects_flowexecutionerrorevent.htm`.

Here are the steps to create a process for the preceding scenario:

1. The first step is to create a custom object called **Exception Messages** to capture flow error messages (see *Figure 6.10*).

    I created a custom object, **Exception Messages**, with fields listed as shown in the following screenshot. This object holds the error messages that can be used by the technical team to troubleshoot issues.

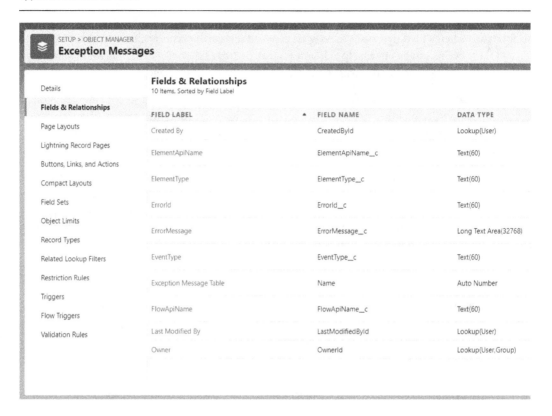

Figure 6.10 - A platform event-triggered flow – the Exception Messages object

We used the standard platform event called **Flow Execution Error Event**: https://developer.salesforce.com/docs/atlas.en-us.platform_events.meta/platform_events/sforce_api_objects_flowexecutionerrorevent.htm

2. Next, we create a platform event-triggered flow using **Flow Execution Error Event** as the **Event** type (see *Figure 6.11*). The flow subscribes to the specified platform's **Flow Execution Error** Event. When a screen flow platform event message is received, the flow is triggered to run.

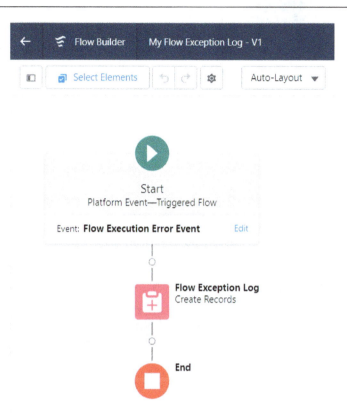

Figure 6.11 - The platform event-triggered flow

Then, we add a create record element called **Flow Exception Log**. We set the field values from the **Flow Execution Error** event that is received to our Exception Messages custom object fields. These values are stored as soon as the **Platform Event** flow completes execution.

3. In the following platform event-triggered flow on the **Edit Create Records** screen, we capture exceptions (errors related to screen flow executions) by assigning them to the fields of a customer object – **Exception Messages**.

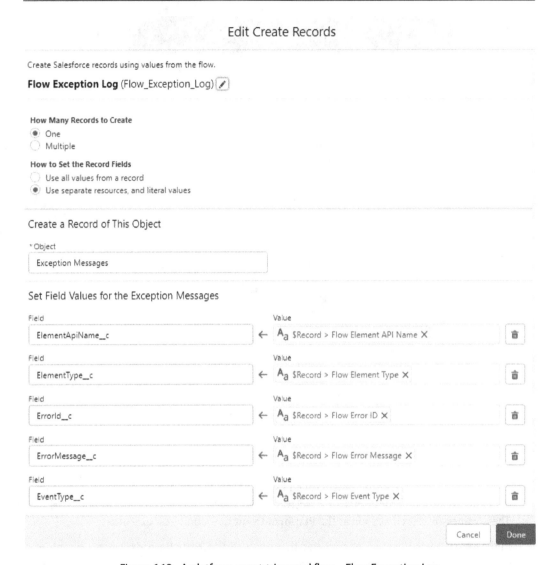

Figure 6.12 - A platform event-triggered flow – Flow Exception Log

Now, let's see our Platform Event-Triggered Flow in action:

1. I created a screen flow to capture the contact's first name, last name, email, and address. I ran the flow and added customer contact information, except for one field on the screen. I purposefully skipped the **Last Name** field to generate a flow exception (see *Figure 6.13*):

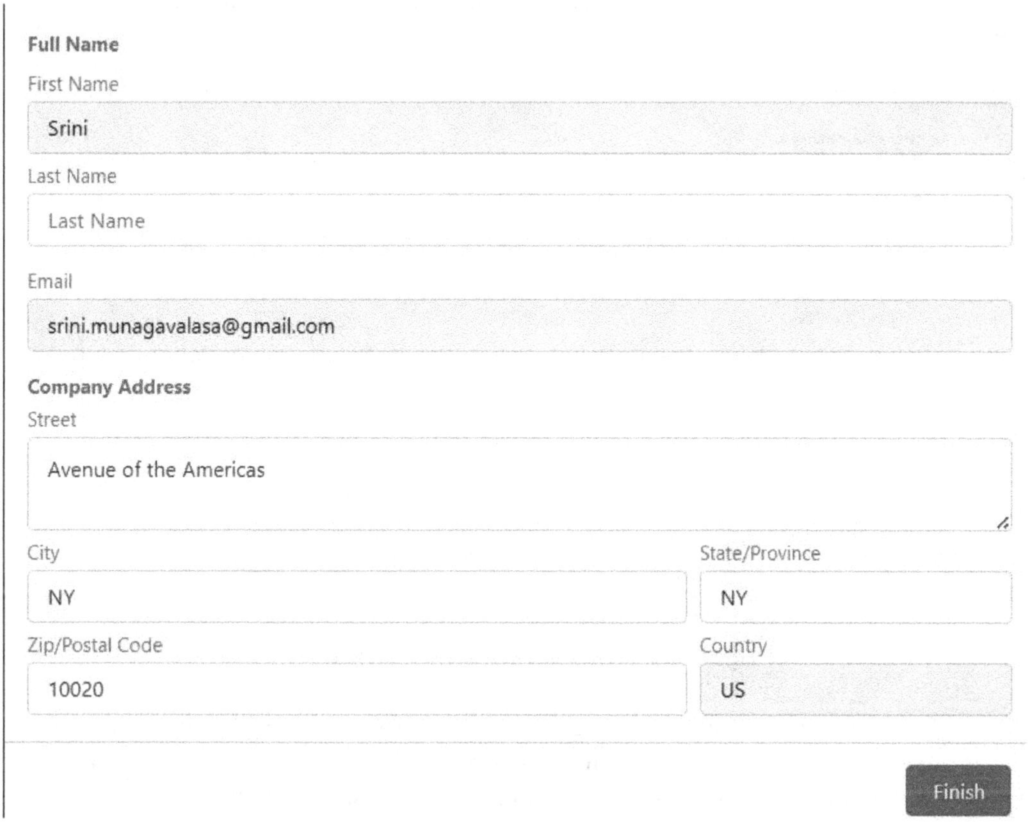

Full Name

First Name

Srini

Last Name

Last Name

Email

srini.munagavalasa@gmail.com

Company Address

Street

Avenue of the Americas

City	State/Province
NY	NY

Zip/Postal Code	Country
10020	US

Finish

Figure 6.13 - A platform event-triggered flow

Since **Last Name** is a mandated field, this flow throws an exception message while creating a contact record. We capture this exception and update the customer object with exception details.

We can see the error message captured as a record in our **Exception Message** object. Your technical team can view these messages from the exception objects periodically and fix the underlying issues. In addition, we can create a record-triggered flow and relay this message via Chatter or email, addressing this error/issue (see *Figure 6.14*).

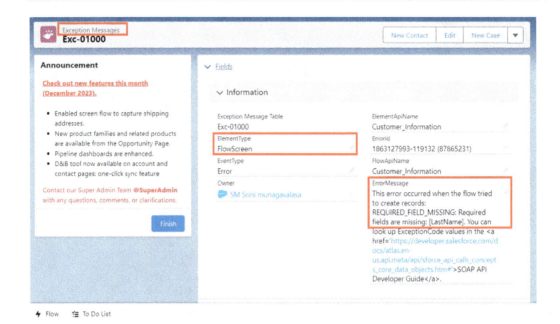

Figure 6.14 - A platform event-triggered flow

2. Another example of a platform event is to publish an event message when the opportunity is closed so that the contract management system (which can be internal or external such as Oracle, SAP, and so on) can subscribe to this custom platform event, initiating the next steps, (i.e., create a contract).

You can create custom platform events from **Setup** | **Integrations** | **Platform Events** | **New Platform Event**.

Click on **New Platform Event** to create your custom event. In the following example, I created a platform event with the **Label** as **Opportunity Won Event**, with two new custom fields called **Opportunity Name** and **Opportunity Stage**.

A platform event structure is like our custom objects (see *Figure 6.15A* and *Figure 6.15B*).

Figure 6.15A - A platform event-triggered flow – Custom Events

3. The API name of the platform event ends with __e. In our case, it would be Opportunity_ Won_Event__e.

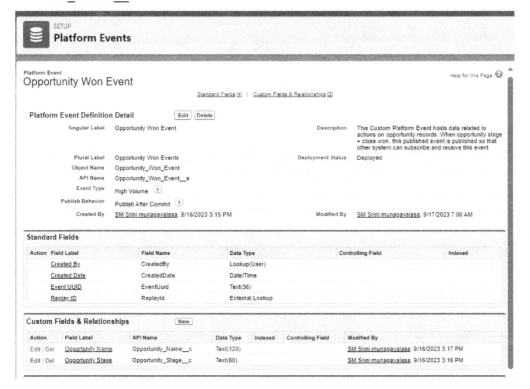

Figure 6.15B - A platform event-triggered flow – sample custom event fields

4. Then, we create a platform event-triggered flow to capture the opportunity attributes when the opportunity is closed (won), and this event data is inserted into our custom platform event object.

    To create the platform event-triggered flow, go to **Setup | Process Automation | Flows | New Flow | Platform Event-Triggered Flow | Create**.

    We will use the custom **Opportunity Won Event** platform event that we created earlier in this section. This flow subscribes to the specified platform event (i.e., **Opportunity Won Event**). When a platform event message is received, this flow is triggered to run. Using a **Create Records** event called **Opportunity Won Platform Event**, we capture platform event messages in the customer object.

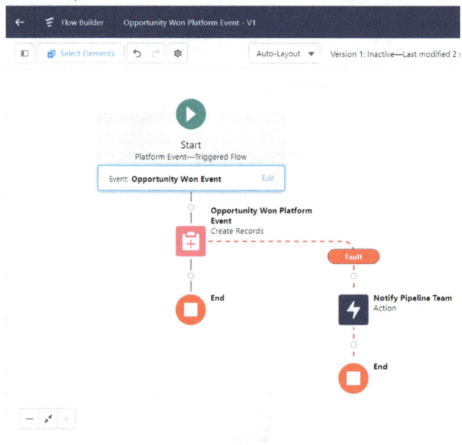

Figure 6.16 - A platform event-triggered flow: Opportunity Won Event

Now that we have seen the power of platform event-triggered flows let's move on to the last of the five flows. After examining flows so far, you may be wondering how a flow can be triggered by something that is not a record change, a schedule, a platform event, or requires no user interaction. Let's explore this in the next section.

An autolaunched flow (no trigger)

This type of flow launches when invoked by Apex, processes, REST API, and so on. The Autolaunched flow runs in the background and is triggered automatically, based on parameters and logic.

An autolaunched flow (no trigger) runs in the background without any input from users. They do not have any triggers defined within the flow. It runs when it is initiated, based on the user's requirements, and they can decide when to trigger this automation.

An autolaunched flow (no trigger) can be triggered from a custom button, another flow such as a sub-flow, or other automations such as Apex code, VF Pages, or an API call from other systems, whereas the other three autolaunched flows run in the background without the user even knowing about that business process automation.

A business scenario for an autolaunched flow (no trigger)

In this scenario, an account manager who had the primary relationship with a customer is able to tag them as a high-value customer (based on criteria such as the number of opportunities during a certain period, the value of those opportunities, and interest in certain emerging products). The account manager will be able to, at their discretion and based on his judgment, launch this feature so that attributes on the account record are updated as per business requirements, as well as create entitlements behind the scenes, such as additional discounts and free premium shipping.

From **Setup**, we go to Flows and create **Autolaunched Flow** (No Trigger). Our account manager, while reviewing data from the account Lightning Console, decided to make this customer a high-value customer so that, from now on, they will get all the premium benefits. This means this flow will update attributes on account records and then update other related records so that, going forward, this high-value customer gets all the premium benefits (see *Figure 6.17*).

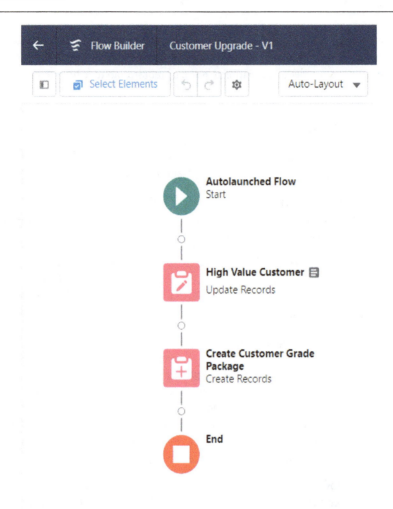

Figure 6.17 - An autolaunched flow (no trigger): Customer Upgrade

Since we want this to be launched at the discretion of the account manager, in this scenario, we created a custom link called **Customer Upgrade** on the **Account** page, under the **Details** section. So, if and when our account manager decides to, they can just click on this link, and our autolaunched flow (no trigger) takes care of business seamlessly behind the scenes (see *Figure 6.18*).

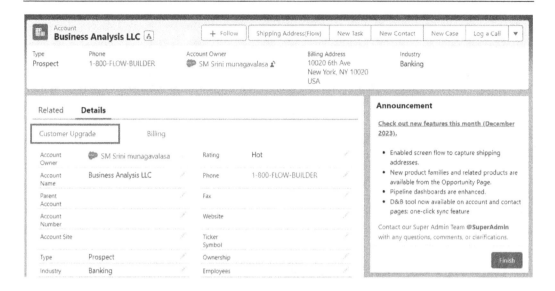

Figure 6.18 - The Customer Upgrade link to trigger our autolaunched flow (no trigger)

You can do the same via a custom button too. Try it out by yourself in one of your dev orgs. Also, did you notice the **Announcement** window on the right side of the screen? This is another example of a screen flow. This is very helpful to communicate with users. How can this be a screen flow when there is no user interaction?

If you have tons of flows in your org, there is an easy way to identify an autolaunched flow (no trigger).

Do you know that we can create list views for flows? With the help of list views, we can easily identify a flow type. A combination of Process Type Trigger mechanisms will provide information related to a flow type.

Flow Type = process type + trigger: As an example, a process type = an autolaunched flow with a trigger = a platform event is a platform event-triggered flow.

Similarly, from the following list view, we can identify an autolaunched flow (no trigger) when **Process Type** is **Autolaunched Flow** and **Trigger** is null (see *Figure 6.19*):

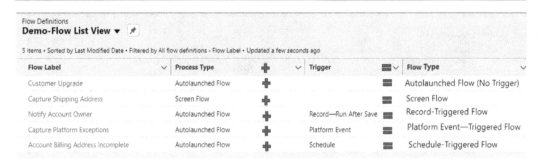

Figure 6.19 - Flow Definitions | Process Type + Trigger = Flow Type

I guess it's time to wrap up this chapter. We discussed all flow types, and now I hope you understand the concepts of why, when, where, and how to enable Salesforce flows to automate your business processes.

Practical tips for flow success

Let's take a look at some practical tips from my experience that you may find useful when implementing various flow types:

- Before you start the development phase of the project, make sure you understand your users' needs; this means you have an approved **Business Requirement Document** (**BRD**) or some kind of prioritized requirements document.

- Flow or no flow, stakeholders and project team members should understand their current and future business processes. This is even more important if you are trying to automate your complex business processes.

- Stagger your automation across multiple releases. Your road map should always try to deliver core functionality, even if it results in some redundancies and manual tasks. These manual tasks can be automated in a future release, based on usability and user feedback.

- Do not automate everything or anything. This does not create a good user experience. Sometimes, users may love interacting with the system to a certain extent so that they can connect to the business processes and get that ownership satisfaction. See my IKEA example in the previous chapter.

- Many times, using AppExchange tools may be a better option rather than trying to automate. So, look out for tools on AppExchange – for example, using the D&B tool to create customers and contacts in Salesforce.

- Just like the way we do for any development or configurations, use standard naming conventions when creating flows with proper descriptions.

- If you are working and updating the same record, use before-save flows (fast field updates). They are faster and more efficient.

- User after-save (actions and related records) if you must do post-save actions, such as posting to Chatter, sending emails, updating related records, or rolling up summaries.

- Always add a path to confirm that a flow is complete, either with a success message or an error message. This will help you get timely information to fix issues in case of failed flows.

- If you are working on automating complex business logic, take the help of your architects and lead developers. In my opinion, flows are 80% clicks and no-code, but for the other 20%, you need to understand the code well. Imagine if you are updating related objects, using platform events, using data manipulations in loops, and so on.

Getting to know practical tips helps us do things right but also saves us valuable project time. I could keep adding more tips, but let's conclude this section here and summarize this chapter.

Summary

This chapter explored the five basic types of flows to automate our business processes. We discussed each flow type in detail with screenshots. We took simplified scenarios and went through explaining each step, looking at concepts and the rationale behind each flow. I hope you now have a better understanding of screen flows, record-triggered flows, schedule-triggered flows, platform event-triggered flows, and autolaunched flows, and how they meet your business needs. With practice, you will be well-equipped to create complex Salesforce flows at your organizations and automate your processes.

In the next chapter, you will learn how to share records via flows that are not available by any other means other than Apex coding. With flow, we have this great feature available where you can perform complex data sharing without resorting to code. You will get to see and explore a real-world business scenario.

Questions

1. Explain the different types of flows.
2. What would be a good use case for a record-triggered flow?
3. How do you differentiate an autolaunched flow (no trigger) from other autolaunched flows?
4. When do we use after-save triggers, and why do we use them?
5. What is the best way to make a screen flow available to users from any page within an app?
6. How do we make flows accessible to your users?

Further reading

- *Screen Flows*: https://trailhead.salesforce.com/content/learn/modules/screen-flows?trail_id=build-flows-with-flow-builder

- *Autolaunched and Scheduled Flows*: https://trailhead.salesforce.com/content/learn/modules/autolaunched-scheduled-flows?trail_id=build-flows-with-flow-builder

- *FlowExecutionErrorEvent*: https://developer.salesforce.com/docs/atlas.en-us.platform_events.meta/platform_events/sforce_api_objects_flowexecutionerrorevent.htm

- *Flow Best Practices*: https://help.salesforce.com/s/articleView?id=sf.flow_prep_bestpractices.htm&type=5

7

Flows Using Apex Sharing

In this chapter, we discuss a very important feature and share records via flows that are not available by any other means other than Apex coding. With Apex sharing, we will be able to write Apex code to share complex and dynamic sharing settings. Now, with flow, we have this feature available where you, as an admin, will be able to perform these actions without code. This topic is a bit advanced for admins. It helps to know that this feature is available in Flow Builder, and a good use case will be to add or remove access to users dynamically.

Before we get into details on flows for Apex sharing, let's quickly recap the different options that we have in Salesforce to share records with your users. We will discuss this in a custom object context only, as Salesforce provides us with the option to have Apex managed sharing via Apex sharing reasons for individual custom objects.

In this chapter, we will cover the following sections:

- Data-sharing options in Salesforce
- Sharing data using Apex managed sharing
- Exploring a real-world business scenario
- Testing out our practical scenario

Even though we say no code, we need to understand code at some level as well as know a few development tools. I will review this in detail with screenshots so that when you plan to do so at your implementation, you will get a good grasp of each step and what it means. I will also take you through testing this scenario step by step, as we need other tools to verify our results.

With this background, let us go to the data-sharing option we currently have in Salesforce in the admin capacity.

Data-sharing options in Salesforce

One of the key requirements for organizations is to have access to and control over business records in their software systems. Your organization should be able to have complete control over who can access your business data. As with all other systems, with Salesforce, you can allow specific users to view an object and restrict the individual records they can see. You can manage record-level access in four ways, and you need a combination of more than one unless you make it public to all objects via **Organization-Wide Defaults (OWD)**.

At a high level, the following are the options to enable access to your users without the need for Apex coding:

- **OWD**: Specifies the default level of access the users can have to each other's data (records). We have three options along with the **Grant Access Using Hierarchies** option. (The **Grant Access Using Hierarchies** option is an OWD setting to control sharing access using hierarchies for any custom object. To make the Salesforce custom object private, disable this option in the OWD setting. It can only be changed for custom objects.)

  - **Private**: Only the owner can access the record if **Grant Access Using Hierarchies** is unchecked; if checked, users above the role hierarchy can access this record.

  - **Public Read Only**: All users can view the record.

  - **Public Read/Write**: All users can edit the record.

- **Role Hierarchy**: Grants access to records owned by users higher in the hierarchy. **Role Hierarchy** is enabled via **Grant Access Using Hierarchies** on OWD. If you check the user above the owner role in the hierarchy, you can access the record.

- **Sharing Rules**: Automatic exceptions and are only used to give additional users access to records. You can share records based on record owner or criteria, and they can be shared with public groups, roles, and subordinates with access levels of read-only or read-write mode.

- **Manual Sharing**: This type of sharing allows owners of particular records to share them with other users. Record owners can set record-level access to individual records manually via account or opportunity teams.

I listed some options here so as to get an idea. In addition, we have default account teams, default opportunity teams, manager groups, implicit sharing, and so on.

Now, let's see if we have a scenario where you would like only a small set of users to be able to access records in a custom object. Can you think of a way to enable this use case using the out-of-the-box features described previously?

Sharing data using Apex managed sharing

Apex managed sharing provides us with the ability to support specific sharing requirements programmatically through Apex or the SOAP API.

We can do this programmatically with the help of technical team members who are conversant with Apex programming, or we can use flows. Flows using Record-Triggered Flow have the ability to access and make changes to Share objects. So, you now have the power to grant or revoke specialized access to users with a click using flows.

> **Note**
>
> Flows using Apex sharing have nothing to do with Apex code. Before flows, we can share records in one of these four ways (OWD, role hierarchy, sharing rules, or manual sharing) with clicks, and the other option is to share records programmatically by using Apex coding. When creating Apex managed sharing, we need to create Apex sharing reasons for individual custom objects to indicate how and why sharing was implemented for the record. Flows use the same feature used by Apex code, and we are repurposing the same Apex sharing reason for flows along with Apex.

Let's see a simple business scenario.

Exploring a real-world business scenario

The business requirement is to create functionality to capture customers' sensitive data for verification. Due to the nature of highly sensitive data, we would like to restrict access to contact record owners and account record owners.

Following are the business requirements in detail:

- Your business requested that they would like to have an object to track contacts' sensitive information such as their tax ID, date of birth, passcode, and signature verification image.

- Only the contact owner and account owner will be able to access these records.

- If the ownership on the contact record is changed, then we need to remove access to prior owners and enable access to new owners.

- The contact owner will get read/write access, whereas the account gets read-only access. For this scenario, we will assume contact and account owners are different.

- Now, with flows, you will be able to enable this dynamic sharing feature without the need for coding.

With these business requirements, we first need a plan. Map this process end to end conceptually. These are the steps we need to take to enable this business requirement:

1. Create a Salesforce object (add a tab and assign it to an app so that users with access can access the records).

2. Create an Apex sharing reason.

3. Make the previously created object private.

4. Create a record-triggered flow on this new object:

    A. Unshare with old owners.

    B. Share with the new owners.

5. Save and activate your flow.

Let's review these steps in detail with screenshots.

Step 1 – Create a Salesforce object

This is the object that holds the contact's sensitive information records.

To create a new object in Salesforce, go to **Setup** | **Create** | **Objects** | **New Custom Object**.

We created a new custom object with labels and fields as listed next. This custom object holds sensitive information and should be shared only with the contact owner and account owner as per the requirements:

- Custom object label = **Contact Sensitive Info**
- Custom fields:

    - **Contact Name**
    - **Contact Sensitive Info Name**
    - **Data of Birth**
    - **Pass Code**
    - **signature verification image**
    - **Tax ID**

Figure 7.1 shows our new custom object called **Contact Sensitive Info**:

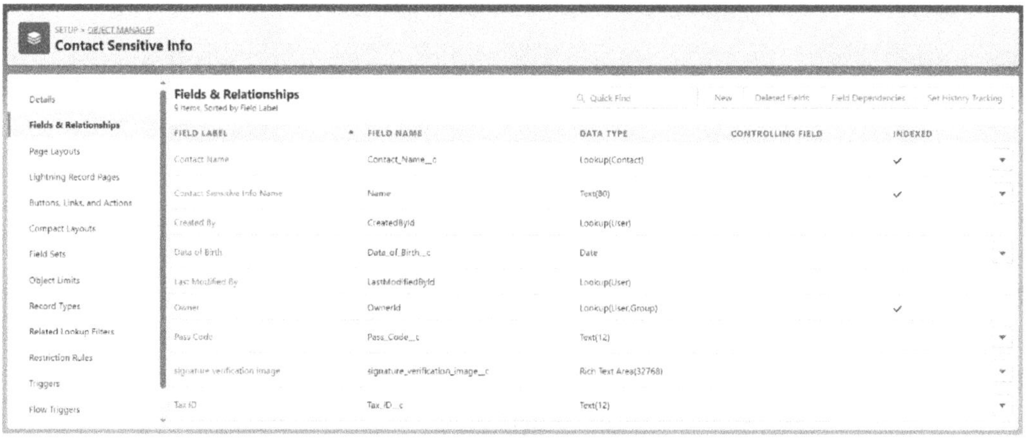

Figure 7.1 – Custom object – Contact Sensitive Info

For simplicity, we will directly add data to this object manually. In reality, we can create a screen-triggered flow to capture input from users.

Step 2 – Create an Apex sharing reason

Create an Apex sharing reason for individual custom objects to indicate the reason for sharing the record. This sharing reason helps technical team members be aware that this record is shared, and they can refer to specific objects when they need to troubleshoot any issues. This used to be in scope for Apex sharing via code before flows. With flows, other team members need to be aware of this feature.

> **Note**
> Apex Sharing Reasons is available in Salesforce Classic mode at the time of writing this chapter.

After we create the object as shown in *Figure 7.1*, scroll down to the **Apex Sharing Reasons**-related list section. To create a new Apex sharing reason, click on **New** and create a new Apex sharing reason, add a **Reason Label** value and a **Reason Name** value, and save your record.

The following screenshot shows the **Apex Sharing Reasons**-related list section on the **Contact Sensitive Info** object.

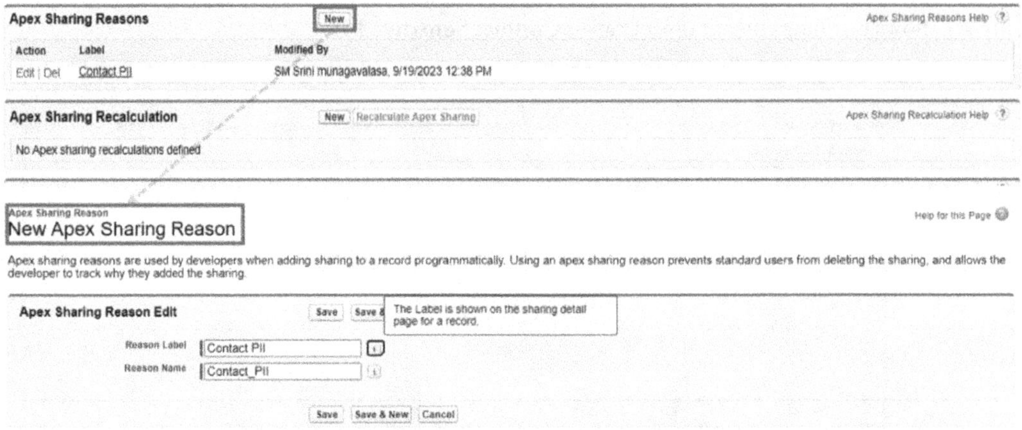

Figure 7.2 – Apex Sharing Reasons section on Contact Sensitive Info object-related list

From here, we create a new Apex sharing reason label, Contact PII. This reason label helps us identify why this record is shared with a user.

Step 3 – Make the object private

Since no one should have access to this record other than the one we wish to share via flow, we need to make this object private from OWD settings.

To access sharing settings for all objects in Salesforce, go to **Setup | Security | Sharing Settings | Organization-Wide Defaults | Edit**:

- For **Object**, add **Contact Sensitive Info**.

- Select **Contact Sensitive Info** and set the access level to **Private**.

- Leave the **Grant Access Using Hierarchies** setting unchecked. Our requirement is not to grant access to records to the users above the role hierarchy:

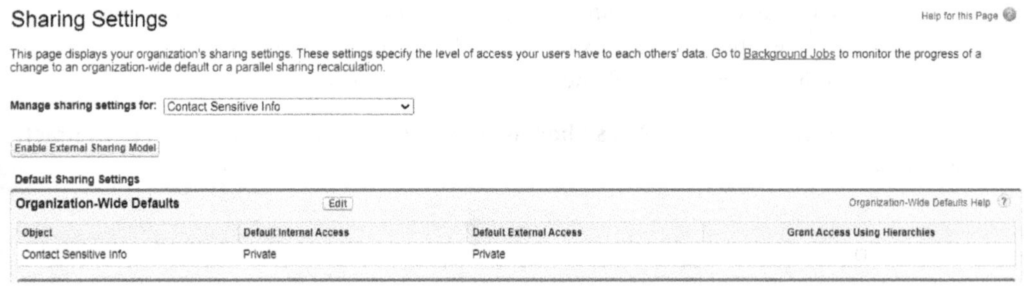

Figure 7.3 – OWD setting for customer object – Contact Sensitive Info

Making a custom object private via OWD will create a sharing object called `<Custom Object>__Share`. In our scenario, it will be `Contact_Sensitive_Info__Share`.

`<Object>__Share` objects are not visible for the Salesforce UI; we need to access them via the Developer Console. See *Figure 7.4.*

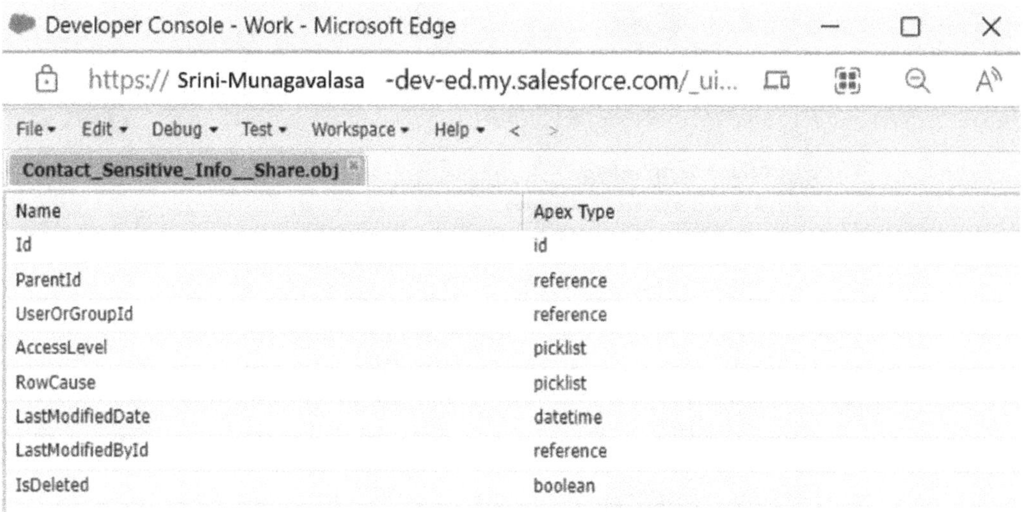

Figure 7.4 – Contact_Sensitive_Info_Share object – the user in this table gets access to a record

To open the Developer Console, click on the gear icon in the right-top corner and select **Developer Console**. In the Query Editor, I added the following query to see the results from the `Contact_Sensitive_Info__Share` object:

```
SELECT Id, ParentId, UserOrGroupId, AccessLevel, RowCause FROM
Contact_Sensitive_Info__Share
```

Our Apex sharing reason label will be captured in the `RowCause` field. This way, technical team members can identify the reason for record sharing with a user.

Step 4 – Create a record-triggered flow on the new object

To create a record-triggered flow, follow these steps:

1. Go to **Flows** and create a new flow.
2. Then, create a record-triggered flow on the object labeled as `Contact Sensitive Info`.
3. Next, we add a **Decision** element to see if the existing record is updated or if it is a new record.
4. Add a **Delete Records** element to remove sharing from the `Contact_Sensitive_Info__Share` object. In this step, we unshare with old owners.

5. Add **Create Records** elements to add the contact owner and account owner to `Contact_Sensitive_Info__Share`. In this step, we share with the new owners.

6. Finally, do not forget to capture exceptions. Use the one that best fits your needs—email, task, Chatter post, and so on:

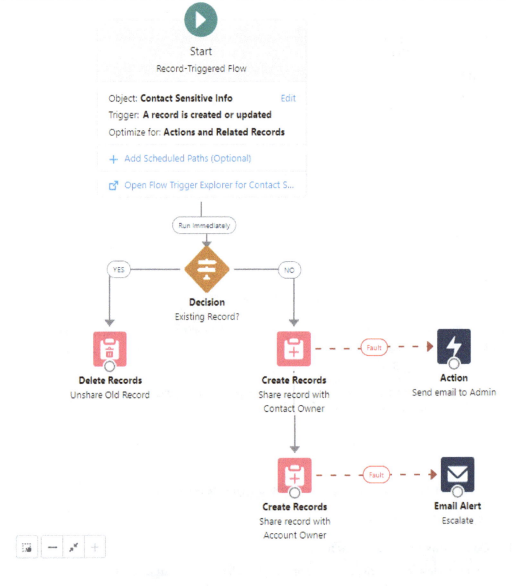

Figure 7.5 – Record-triggered flow on Contact Sensitive Info object

Last step – Click on the Save button and name your flow

Click on the **Save** button and in the **Flow Label** field, enter `Contact Sensitive Info`.

So far, we have created all the necessary parts to enable Apex sharing functionality via flows. Let's see this in action in the next section.

Testing out our practical scenario

To test out the functionality, let's open the **Contact Sensitive Info** custom object.

As an admin, I created a record on the **Contact Sensitive Info** object, as shown in *Figure 7.6*. I added **Tax ID**, **Data of Birth**, **Pass Code**, and **signature verification image** values for the existing contact record, **King Valkyrie**. Let's call this record **King Valkyrie_PII Data**.

After I save this record, our record-triggered flow fires and completes, granting access to users to this new record. Now, these users will have access to this sensitive information record. Optionally, you can add notifications to these users from the flow:

Figure 7.6 - Contact Sensitive Info page (sample record)

We would like to grant access to only a limited number of users. Let's see who has access to this **King Valkyrie_PII Data** record.

Our requirement is to grant access only to **Contact Owner** and **Account Owner** (see *Figure 7.7*) and no one else. Remember – the record owner will also get access to the record. If the admin creates data for the contact owner, change the owner to the record after creating the record:

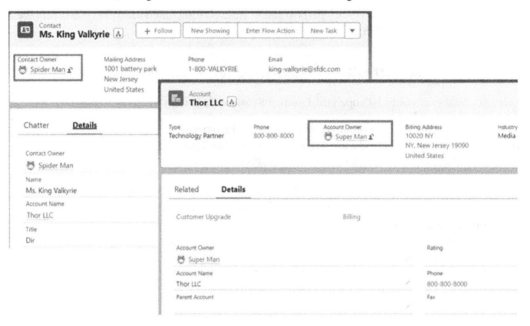

Figure 7.7 - Contact and account records related to Contact Sensitive Info record

Now, let's see who can access this **Contact Sensitive Info** record:

1. From the **Contact Sensitive Info** record, click on **Sharing from Quick Actions**. (If you do not see it, enable it on your Lightning page – refer to *Empower Your Users with Quick Actions Unit | Salesforce Trailhead*: `https://trailhead.salesforce.com/content/learn/modules/lex_customization/lex_customization_actions`).

2. You can see that this record is shared with the following:

    *   **Contact owner: Spider-Man—Read/Write**

    *   **Account owner: Super Man—Read Only**

    *   **Record owner: SM-Srini munagavalasa**—Full access:

Figure 7.8 - Contact Sensitive Info record Share screen

3. You can see more details using the Developer Console. Look at the RowCause column on the Share object – Contact_Sensitive_Info__Share. You can display results with a simple SOQL query:

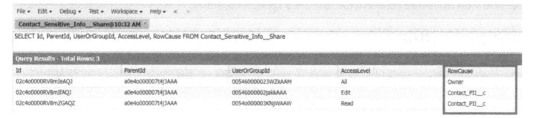

Figure 7.9 - Entries for our record in Contact_Sensitive_Info_Share object

We can successfully test our Flow and Apex sharing records with only restricted users as required by business needs. It may be overwhelming to you, as we used some core developer skills in this chapter. This is a very powerful feature, and by understanding development concepts, you will be able to create functionality with flows. Think of a similar scenario at work and try to implement it in one of your development boxes. With this, let's summarize this chapter.

Summary

In this chapter, you got exposed to a unique flow feature that can help us enhance functionality and at the same time automate it. Apex sharing using code follows the same steps as laid out in this chapter, except for Apex code, which we replace with flows.

You learned how to create an Apex sharing reason and how it is useful to grant and/or revoke access to your users for special-case records. You saw how we can update the Share objects using a record-triggered flow. Finally, we saw a real-world example and were able to verify how the data got updated on our Share objects.

For this, you need a deeper understanding of sharing objects and using Workbench and the Developer Console. You need a little bit of practice to get the hang of it. Keep practicing; you will enjoy it.

In the next chapter, we will explore and learn how to use the Flow Builder debug window. We often run into some kind of issue, and you need a tool to be able to understand and find the root cause. We will also discuss a few scenarios and understand the concepts better.

Questions

1. What is the benefit of using flows to share records? And why?
2. How do we identify the reason for record sharing with a user?
3. How do we revoke access to the user for a specific record?

Further reading

- *Understanding Sharing | Apex Developer Guide | Salesforce Developers*: `https://developer.salesforce.com/docs/atlas.en-us.apexcode.meta/apexcode/apex_bulk_sharing_understanding.htm`

- *Workbench* (`developerforce.com`): `https://workbench.developerforce.com/login.php`

8

Optimizing and Troubleshooting Flows

So far, we have learned the building blocks of **Flow Builder**, understood the intricacies of various flow types, and observed the power of Salesforce flows. We gained insight into how to transform and automate business needs and processes and create an amazing user experience. Now, it is time to ensure that your flows are optimized, working as intended with minimal or no issues, and meeting your business needs.

In this chapter, we will explore and learn how to use the Flow Builder debug window to optimize and troubleshoot flows. Anything developed either declaratively or using code will run into some kind of bug, and you need a tool to be able to understand the error message and what it means. We will discuss a few scenarios to effectively debug and make sense of the flow for the users.

In this chapter, we will cover the following sections:

- Learning about the Flow debug window
- Understanding flow errors
- Practical scenario – failed flow example
- Flow tips

As we know, as with any development work, flows contain elements that interact with Salesforce objects. This means there is some action on the database to create, update, or delete records. These interactions with the database may sometimes fail. When flows fail, the default error messages are cryptic and confusing. This chapter discusses how to identify faults in your flows before they are deployed and find ways to communicate these error messages to your users in a sensible way when faults happen in your production system. At some point, errors are bound to happen due to faults in your flows; let's see how we can mitigate them.

Let's learn about flow debugging in Flow Builder.

Learning about the flow debug window

Debugging from Flow Builder can be done with simple clicks. We do not need to create debug logs using trace flags and then go through **debug log details**.

> **What are debug logs?**
>
> A debug log records database operations and system processes such as validations, assignment rules, and so on, and any errors while executing a transaction. The system generates a debug log for a user to execute a transaction. You can specify a trace flag with start and expiration dates that contain the transaction's start time. Debugging logs gives greater details, and you need to have a good level of technical skills to be able to interpret these logs.

Flow debug is not just to be used when we run into issues. This is an extremely helpful tool for us to test chunks of functionality and make sure it works end to end as desired. The debug window captures details that let us see how our flow flows. This provides step-by-step results on how well the flow has been executed—how it is triggered, which actions are taking place, and the outcome. We can fine-tune our steps in the flow and fix any faults, optimize individual steps, customize error messages, add information messages, and so on.

Let's look at the key features of the debug window.

The following are the steps from start to finish:

1. To access flow debug, open the flow in Flow Builder.
2. Click **Debug**.
3. Set the debug options and input variables.
4. Scroll through screens (if you have multiple screens) by clicking **Next**, and end the flow by selecting **Finish** on the last screen.
5. You can debug the flow again with the same input values or by changing input values:

   A. **Change Inputs**: Select this to debug the flow with different scenarios (input values).

   B. **Run Again**: Select this to rerun with the same inputs.

Simple practical scenario – capture shipping address

The analyst will be able to capture the shipping address using **Screen Flow**.

Let's walk through a happy path scenario. In this scenario, everything works magically as desired. Make sure we enter valid values so that our flow works from start to finish.

Let's review the scenario that we discussed in *Chapter 6*.

This is our business process flow:

1. The user goes to the account screen.

2. Access and run the screen flow.

3. If the shipping address is the same as the billing address, copy the billing address to the shipping address.

4. If not, collect and input the shipping address.

5. Save the record.

6. Display a success or error message on the screen.

We used **Screen Flow** to enable this functionality. In our scenario, in this section, we will test this functionality from Flow Builder itself.

Open your flow (in our example, it is **Screen Flow: Shipping Address Update**, as shown in *Figure 8.1*) and click on **Debug**:

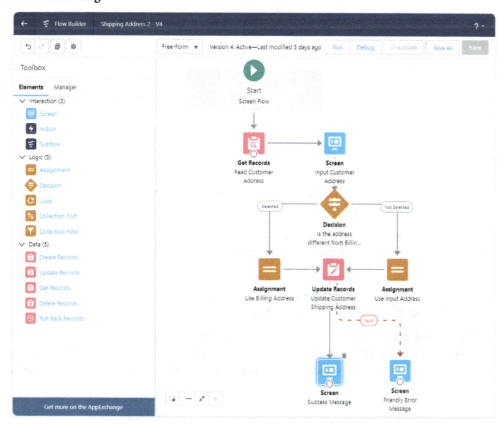

Figure 8.1 – Screen Flow: Shipping Address Update

The **Debug** button on the flow opens the **Debug flow** window. Here, we can set the debug options and input variables, as shown in *Figure 8.2*:

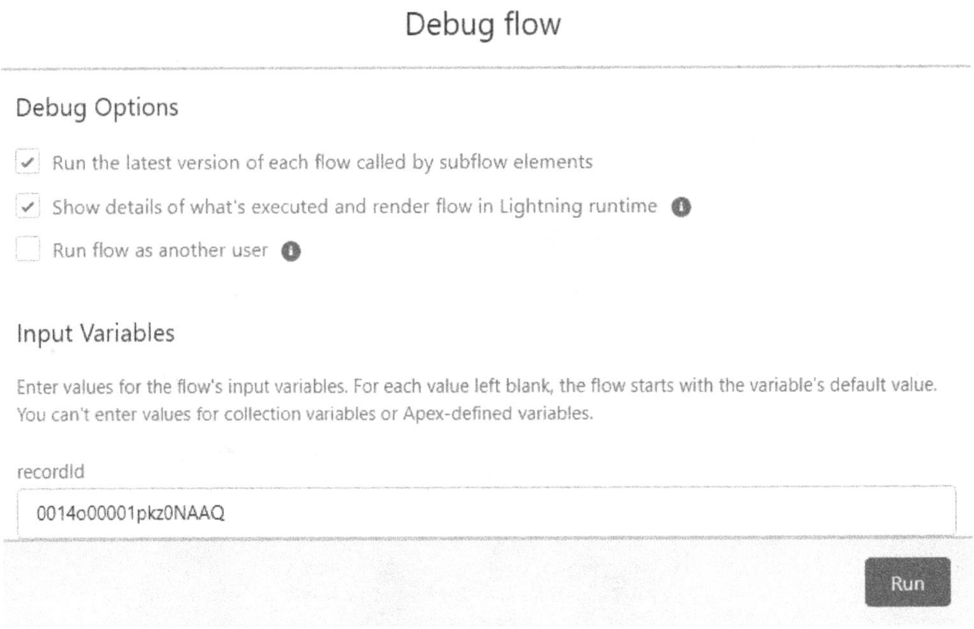

Debug flow

Debug Options

☑ Run the latest version of each flow called by subflow elements

☑ Show details of what's executed and render flow in Lightning runtime ⓘ

☐ Run flow as another user ⓘ

Input Variables

Enter values for the flow's input variables. For each value left blank, the flow starts with the variable's default value. You can't enter values for collection variables or Apex-defined variables.

recordId

0014o00001pkz0NAAQ

Run

Figure 8.2 – Debug flow window

We have the following options:

- Run the latest version. This is mostly the case unless you have specific conditions where you need to test older versions.

- Show details of what's executed and render flow in the Lightning runtime. I checked this so that I can see the details of the steps of flow execution.

- Run the flow as another user. Make sure you debug this as different personas. As an admin, you will have full access to Salesforce, and you may not run into any issues. Many a time, the main culprit may be your user's access to data.

- **Input variables**: These are the `recordId` variables of the record that trigger the screen flow. For our users, we supply this via a **Custom** button, a custom URL, and so on. Since we are simulating this in Flow Builder, we need to provide this record ID. In our example, this will be our 18-character ID of the account record.

To execute your flow, click on **Run**. This will start the flow interview. A **flow interview** is a runtime instance of a flow. If the flow is your Salesforce object, then the flow instance is a record in that object.

Since this is a screen flow, you are presented with a screen. In our case, we just have one, but in practice, for complex implementations, we will have multiple screens.

Input values on the screen as per the scenario you plan to verify. You need to debug multiple scenarios with different combinations. In *Figure 8.3*, you will see the flow of action.

The right side of the screen, **Debug Details**, is where you see step-by-step flow execution.

It starts with how the flow interview started—who started it, the API version, and flow variables.

In the other scenario, we did the following:

1. We provided the `recordId` variables for our account record.

2. Next, we used the **GET RECORDS** element to get billing and shipping address data from the account object with the **account ID** as `recordId` that we supplied earlier.

3. Debug details confirm these results. The flow interview will display if the transaction was completed successfully or failed.

4. Next, we see the **Transaction Committed** statement. In our case, it is just reading data; no commit happens.

Now, it's time to input data on the screen:

1. If we decide to copy the billing address, all we need to do is select the checkbox, as shown in *Figure 8.3*.

2. But let us pick a scenario where we would like to capture a shipping address that is different from the billing address, so I input address details and click on **Next**. If we have more screens, the flow interview will display the next screen for input:

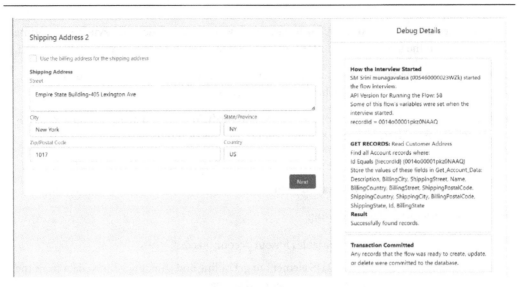

Figure 8.3 – Flow in action: flow interview start

3. Since we have just a single screen, clicking on the **Next** button displays a success message. This is a custom message for our users displayed via a screen element. This action completes the transaction and saves the shipping address to the account record.

4. Now, click on **Finish** to complete the flow interview:

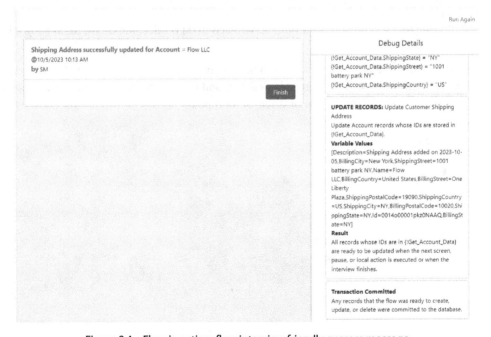

Figure 8.4 – Flow in action: flow interview friendly success message

5. The **Finish** action in the prior step displays the message that the interview is finished with a date and time stamp. This message is now captured in the **Debug Details** section.

6. From this all-done screen, we have the option to change inputs, which means you can run a flow for a different record ID (in our case, another account), as well as other users' values and different screen input values, and test other variations. Also, you can run the flow again, which lets you rerun or run different screen inputs for the same record (see *Figure 8.5*):

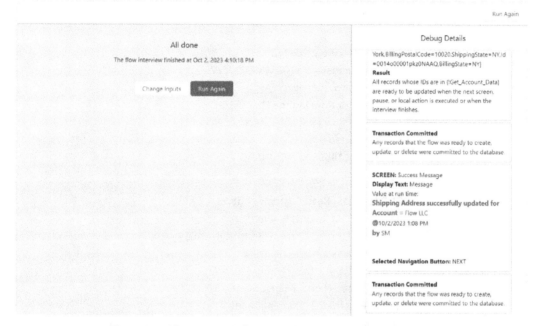

Figure 8.5 – Flow in action: flow interview end (successful scenario)

So far, we looked at the flow UI from the users' perspective and input fields to capture shipping address information. To get insight, let us review the debug details in a bit more detail.

Typical steps in the Debug Details window

This window is visible on the right side of your screen. We will quickly review each of these subsections:

- **How the Interview Started**: This is the first section where you can see information related to the following:

   A. Running user

   B. API version

   C. Record ID used for triggering the flow

- **GET RECORDS**: Flow element to read customer addresses It uses a query to get all account records that meet the input criteria. Since the account ID is unique, we only have one record as output. For complex screen flows, you may have to retrieve multiple records and create a flow to handle multiple records:

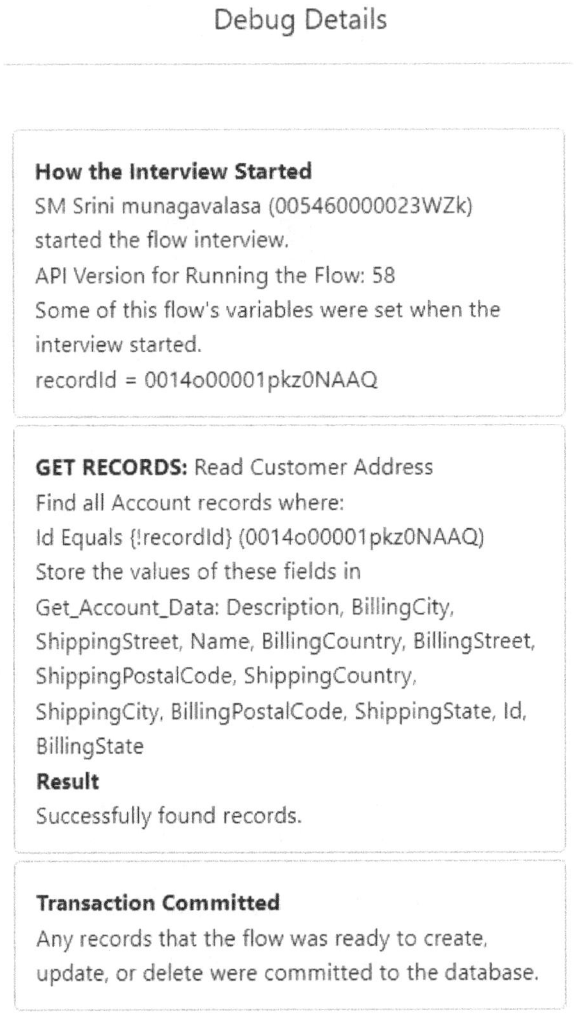

Debug Details

How the Interview Started

SM Srini munagavalasa (005460000023WZk) started the flow interview.

API Version for Running the Flow: 58

Some of this flow's variables were set when the interview started.

recordId = 0014o00001pkz0NAAQ

GET RECORDS: Read Customer Address

Find all Account records where:

Id Equals {!recordId} (0014o00001pkz0NAAQ)

Store the values of these fields in

Get_Account_Data: Description, BillingCity, ShippingStreet, Name, BillingCountry, BillingStreet, ShippingPostalCode, ShippingCountry, ShippingCity, BillingPostalCode, ShippingState, Id, BillingState

Result

Successfully found records.

Transaction Committed

Any records that the flow was ready to create, update, or delete were committed to the database.

Figure 8.6A – Interview start

- **SCREEN: Input Customer Address**: Here, the **Input Customer Address** screen element will be rendered for input.

- **DECISION: Is the address different from Billing Address?**: This decision element will let us decide if it is or is not different from the billing address. In our case, it is **false**, which means we do not want the billing address copied to the shipping address:

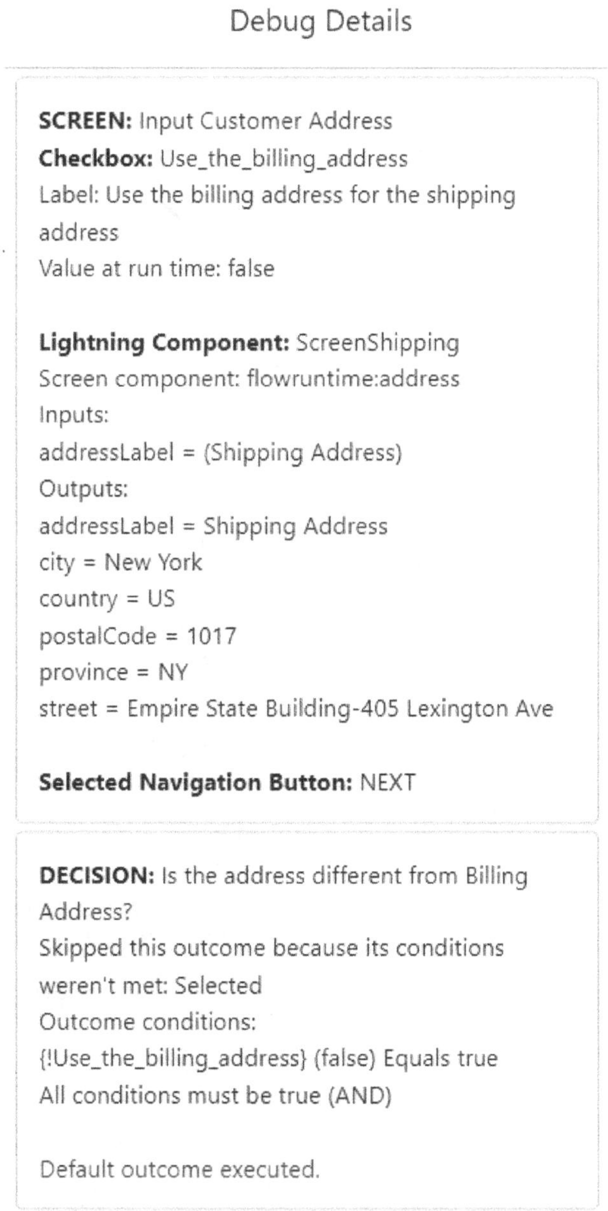

Debug Details

SCREEN: Input Customer Address
Checkbox: Use_the_billing_address
Label: Use the billing address for the shipping address
Value at run time: false

Lightning Component: ScreenShipping
Screen component: flowruntime:address
Inputs:
addressLabel = (Shipping Address)
Outputs:
addressLabel = Shipping Address
city = New York
country = US
postalCode = 1017
province = NY
street = Empire State Building-405 Lexington Ave

Selected Navigation Button: NEXT

DECISION: Is the address different from Billing Address?
Skipped this outcome because its conditions weren't met: Selected
Outcome conditions:
{!Use_the_billing_address} (false) Equals true
All conditions must be true (AND)

Default outcome executed.

Figure 8.6B – Interview: input screen and decision elements

- **ASSIGNMENT: Use Input Address**: Based on the decision to capture the shipping address, the screen input values are assigned to the variables:

Debug Details

ASSIGNMENT: Use Input Address
{!Get_Account_Data.ShippingCity} Equals
{!ScreenShipping.city}
{!Get_Account_Data.ShippingCountry} Equals
{!ScreenShipping.country}
{!Get_Account_Data.ShippingPostalCode} Equals
{!ScreenShipping.postalCode}
{!Get_Account_Data.ShippingState} Equals
{!ScreenShipping.province}
{!Get_Account_Data.ShippingStreet} Equals
{!ScreenShipping.street}
Result
{!Get_Account_Data.ShippingCity} = "New York"
{!Get_Account_Data.ShippingPostalCode} = "1017"
{!Get_Account_Data.ShippingState} = "NY"
{!Get_Account_Data.ShippingStreet} = "Empire
State Building-405 Lexington Ave"
{!Get_Account_Data.ShippingCountry} = "US"

Figure 8.6C – Interview and assignments

- **UPDATE RECORDS: Update Customer Shipping Address**: We take the preceding assignment values and save them to the database using the **UPDATE RECORDS** data element.

- **Transaction Committed**: Since we did not encounter any errors or issues, the new shipping address was saved to the account record successfully:

Debug Details

UPDATE RECORDS: Update Customer Shipping Address
Update Account records whose IDs are stored in {!Get_Account_Data}.
Variable Values
[Description=Shipping Address added on 2023-10-02,BillingCity=New York,ShippingStreet=Empire State Building-405 Lexington Ave,Name=Flow LLC,BillingCountry=United States,BillingStreet=1260 Avenue Of The Americas,ShippingPostalCode=1017,ShippingCountry=US,ShippingCity=New York,BillingPostalCode=10020,ShippingState=NY,Id=0014o00001pkz0NAAQ,BillingState=NY]
Result
All records whose IDs are in {!Get_Account_Data} are ready to be updated when the next screen, pause, or local action is executed or when the interview finishes.

Transaction Committed
Any records that the flow was ready to create, update, or delete were committed to the database.

Figure 8.6D – Interview: record update

- **SCREEN: Success Message:** Here, we display a custom success message. We use a screen element to display this on the screen for the users:

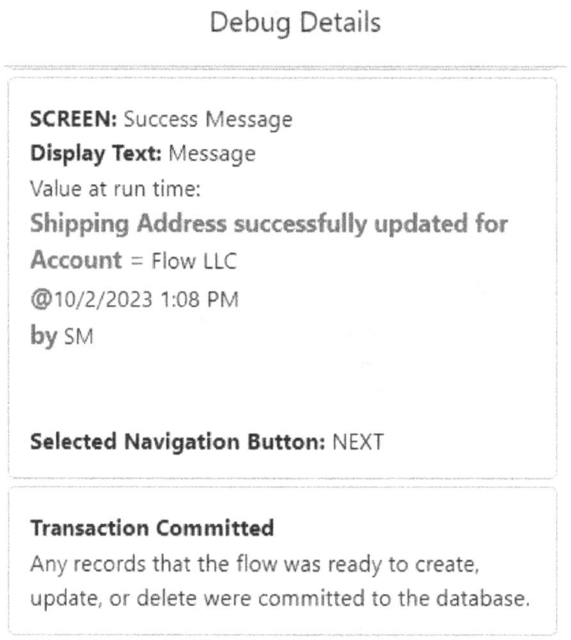

Debug Details

SCREEN: Success Message
Display Text: Message
Value at run time:
Shipping Address successfully updated for
Account = Flow LLC
@10/2/2023 1:08 PM
by SM

Selected Navigation Button: NEXT

Transaction Committed
Any records that the flow was ready to create,
update, or delete were committed to the database.

Figure 8.6E – Interview completed

I hope you now get a sense of how the flow runs and can see each executed step with granular details. It is available within Flow Builder and is easy to read and understand. You will exactly know where and why it failed.

In the next section, let's understand the error messages that we may likely encounter while executing flows.

Understanding flow errors

So far, we have seen a happy path and understood how our flow behaves. But even with due diligence and thorough planning and testing, there will always be some scenarios and edge cases that are bound to fail and cause nightmares for your team.

If we do not plan and design our flow, users will run into exceptions with no information on why they failed or some cryptic message that no one can understand. What do they do now? Get frustrated?

To remediate this problem, we need to plan for these exceptions. Issues will happen, and if we are prepared to handle them promptly and fix the root cause, we will create a better user experience.

We can enable this in more than one way:

- By displaying a custom-specific error message and informing the users exactly what caused the issue, they can fix the issue and retry. For example, we can notify the users that certain fields are not accurately populated, or a specific value is invalid.

- For an auto-triggered flow, we often see error messages such as **An unhandled fault has occurred in this flow**, and the user does not have control over the flow. See *Figure 8.6F*. We can handle these errors by configuring fault paths for each flow element. As a best practice, Salesforce recommends that we configure the fault connectors in our flows to receive an email notification when our flow fails:

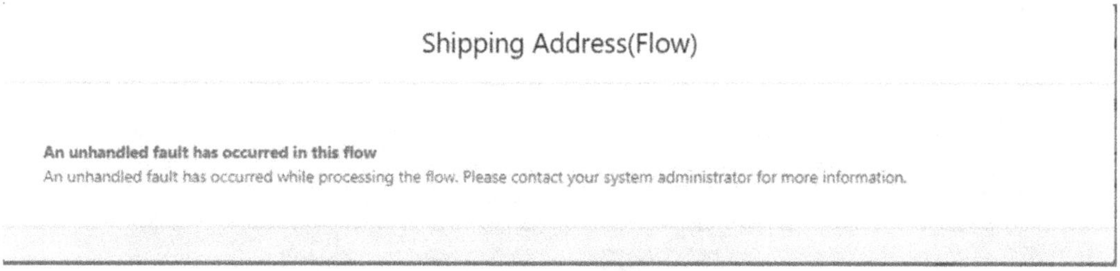

Shipping Address(Flow)

An unhandled fault has occurred in this flow
An unhandled fault has occurred while processing the flow. Please contact your system administrator for more information.

Figure 8.6F – Unhandled flow fault system message

- **Request corrections on screen**: Add a fault connector to the screen so that your users can confirm and verify the data.

- Display a user-friendly error message by drawing the fault connector to a screen element with helpful text fields.

- Display a friendly error message to your users and notify them that a case has been created. Provide the case number in the message. In the background, create a case with a fault message and all the resource variable details, and assign the case to your admin or production support team. See *Figure 8.6G*:

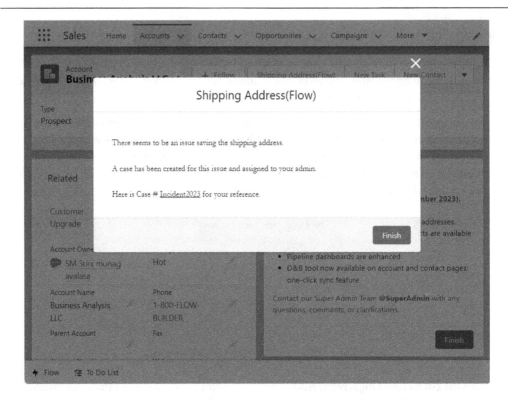

Figure 8.6G – User-friendly flow fault message

> **Creating a case or sending flow error notifications**
>
> This is a best practice that helps the admin know what happened to the flow. Rather than waiting for your user to notify us about the issue, we can do this by creating a text template and including the values of all flow resources. This will help us see the values the user entered on screen flows and, for other autolaunched flows, the exact value of flow variables in case the interview fails.

Now that we have seen an end-to-end debug detail, I hope you have a good idea of how to test your flows by using the flow debug feature that is available from Flow Builder. Even with the best of intentions and efforts, there is always a chance that your users may run into issues post-deployment. This is where the email that gets generated when the flow interview fails provides us with granular details so that our technical team will be able to troubleshoot, do a **root cause analysis** (**RCA**), and fix the issue.

Troubleshooting flow errors

If a flow interview fails, Salesforce notifies the admin and the recipients of the relevant flow last modifier or Apex exception email. Configure this feature so that a member of your admin/technical team is contacted as soon as a user discovers flow issues.

The email is included in *Figure 8.7*:

Subject: Error Occurred During Flow "Lead_to_Contact Demo Flow":
This error occurred when the flow tried to create ...

 FlowApplication <info@jp.salesforce.com>
to srini.munagavalasa@gmail.com

You are viewing an attached message. Gmail can't verify the authenticity of attached messages.

Debug the failed interview in Flow Builder for the interview GUID: 609532f6a7cbe0a0a7ff3551759718af670a333-3adb

Error element Create_Contact_from_Lead (FlowRecordCreate).
This error occurred when the flow tried to create records: REQUIRED_FIELD_MISSING: Required fields are missing: [Security_ID__c].
You can look up ExceptionCode values in the SOAP API Developer Guide.

Flow Details
Flow API Name: Lead_to_Contact_Demo_Flow
Type: Autolaunched Flow
Version: 3
Status: Active
Org: mufg (00D4600000113Dg)

Flow Interview Details
Interview Label: Lead_to_Contact Demo Flow 10/3/2023 1:03 PM
Interview GUID: 609532f6a7cbe0a0a7ff3551759718af670a333-3adb
Current User: SM Srini munagavalasa (005460000023WZk)
Start time: 10/3/2023 1:03 PM
Duration: 0 seconds

How the Interview Started
This debug run was triggered as if the lead record was created.
SM Srini munagavalasa (005460000023WZk) started the flow interview.
API Version for Running the Flow: 58
Some of this flow's variables were set when the interview started.
$Record = Lead (00Q4600000LpNFEEA3)

START CONDITION REQUIREMENTS:
The triggering record met the condition requirements.
Entry Conditions
1. Status (Working - Contacted) Equals Working - Contacted
2. AnnualRevenue (2000000.0) Greater than 1000000.0
Logic: All conditions must be true (AND)

CREATE RECORDS: Create Contact from Lead
Create one Contact record where:
Department = Sales
Email = {!$Record.Email} (dr.hello@universe.llc)
FirstName = {!$Record.FirstName} (Hello)
LastName = {!$Record.LastName} (World)
MailingCity = {!$Record.City} (New York)
MailingCountry = {!$Record.Country} (USA)
MailingPostalCode = {!$Record.PostalCode} (100001)
MailingState = {!$Record.State} (NY)
MailingStreet = {!$Record.Street} (1001 battery park)
Result
Failed to create record.

Error Occurred: This error occurred when the flow tried to create records:
REQUIRED_FIELD_MISSING: Required fields are missing: [Security_ID__c].
You can look up ExceptionCode values in the SOAP API Developer Guide.

Transaction Rolled Back
Because an error occurred, any records that the flow was ready to create, update, or delete weren't committed to the database.

Salesforce Error ID: 648870654-37446 (513353057)

Figure 8.7 – Failed flow email message details (sample email notification to admin)

As you can see from the preceding screenshot, there is the following:

- An error message
- Details of the flow elements executed by the interview
- A link to view the failed flow interview in Flow Builder

There are a few troubleshooting options to fix these user errors. Most of them can be fixed relatively quickly. You need to be aware of what they are and at what point in the flow they happen.

Troubleshooting options

Most flow issues can be proactively or timely addressed if you keep allocating enough time to take care of the following options:

1. The **Debug** option in Flow Builder is our best option. We can see real-time details of what the flow does. We can set input variables and restart the flow as needed. Try different scenarios by changing input values and running users where applicable.

2. **Flow URLs**: We may be distributing our flow via a **Custom** button or custom link; check the underlying flow. In most cases, you may not be passing the right variable to the underlying flow or changes made to the flow, and the new version is not activated. Also, if you rename the flow, make sure the flow's new API name is used by the flow URL.

3. **Process error email recipients**: When flow interviews fail, a detailed email is generated and sent to the admin who last modified the flow. Send it to your Level-3 support or technical team so that they will be in a better position to resolve them more efficiently and efficiently.

> **Note**
>
> To configure Apex exceptions, email recipients as follows:
>
> - From **Setup | Process Automation Settings**, set **Send Process** or **Flow Error Email** to **Apex Exception Email Recipients**.
> - From **Setup | Email | Apex Exception Email**, set a Salesforce user email or external email address.

> **Important note**
>
> **Do not** use the browser's **Back** button to navigate through a flow. Doing so can cause inconsistent data between the flow and Salesforce.

Now that we've learned about flow errors and how to troubleshoot them, let's look at a simplified practical scenario.

Practical scenario – failed flow example

I purposely introduced a few errors in the flow so that we could review and get a good understanding.

Scenario: When the lead is updated to status = Working-Contacted and annual revenue is greater than $1 million, create a contact. We need to add a required field called security on contact via flow, and it should be 10 characters. We will hardcode this value in the flow for testing different variants.

Create a record-triggered flow with two conditions: status = Working-Contact and annual revenue greater than 1 million.

This triggered flow runs immediately when the preceding conditions are met and a lead is updated. See *Figure 8.8*:

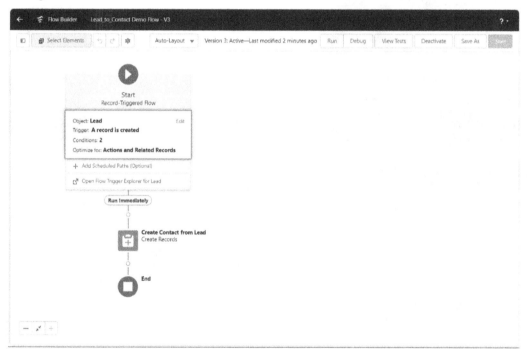

Figure 8.8 – Record-triggered flow: Lead to Contact flow

Start the interview flow by clicking on **Debug**. This opens the **Debug flow** window; see *Figure 8.9*. The flow runs immediately and in **rollback mode**. This means that the flow debug process ensures that when the flow process ends, any operation on the database, such as create, update, or delete, is rolled back and not committed to the database. This is disabled by default, and we do have only a rollback option in debug mode. This ensures no data is saved to the database.

I added an existing lead, and the data from this lead will be utilized to run the flow (see *Figure 8.9*):

Set the Lead name as `Hello World`.

I created a contact with the same last name and email as the lead. This is to catch duplicate exceptions in the flow debug:

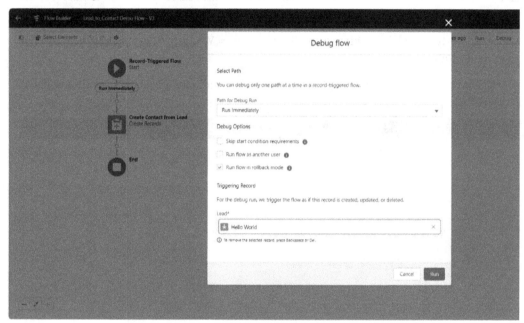

Figure 8.9 – Lead to Contact: Debug flow window

After clicking on **Run**, the entry condition is met, and creating a record element in the flow is executed. As I said earlier, since there was a contact with the same last name and email, the flow errored as there was a duplicate contact record, and the execution ended. See *Figure 8.10*. We can see a *NO* icon next to the element where the flow failed:

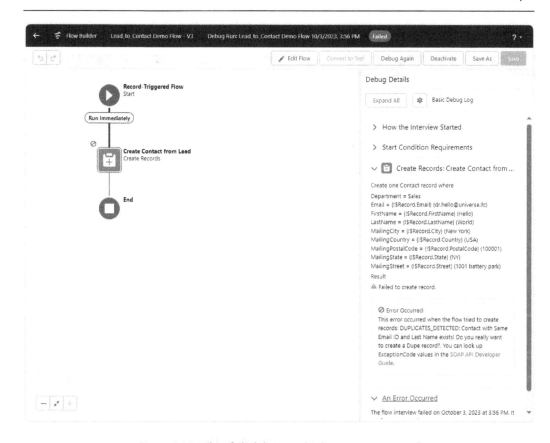

Figure 8.10 – Flow failed due to a duplicate contact record

I fixed the duplicate contact issue and reran the flow for the same lead. But then I removed the hardcoded value for the security field, and this field is required to create a contact.

From *Figure 8:11*, you can see the flow failed, as the required field is missing:

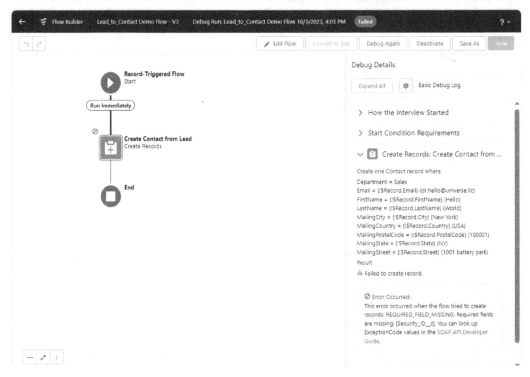

Figure 8.11 – Flow failed due to the required field missing

I added hardcoded values for the security field with more than a 10-character limit.

From *Figure 8.12*, you can see the flow failed as the string is too long:

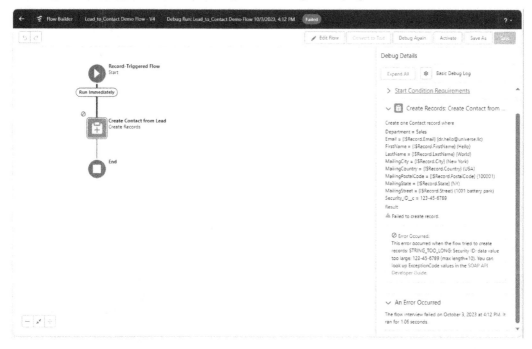

Figure 8.12 – Flow failed due to the required field length being too long

After fixing the string length and rerunning the flow with the same lead, the flow ran successfully without any errors. See *Figure 8.13*. Contact record creation was rolled back:

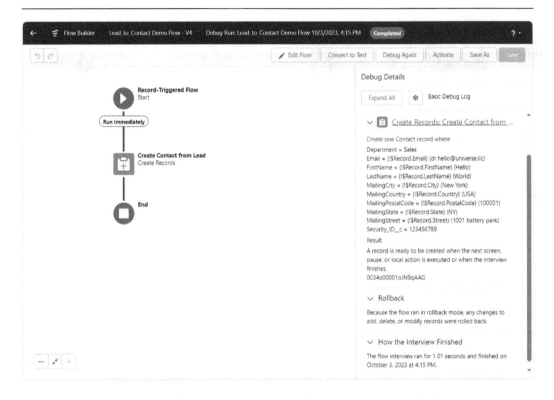

Figure 8.13 – Flow interview finished successfully

Play with the flow debug tool in the developer box to get a feel for it. You will be able to manipulate a variable and see how it behaves. You can also understand the flow process better and be able to fine-tune and optimize your flows.

Let's see some important flow limits. Knowing the limits will help you design your flows better.

Flow tips

At a high level, as an administrator, you need to consider the following when designing flows:

- Flows launched by another flow via a sub-flow element count as one flow interview.
- Flows from managed packages cannot be opened.
- Session timeouts will impact your flows; if the user session expires, flows in progress are interrupted and cannot be resumed.
- Publicly accessible screen input fields should not be mapped to rich text fields to prevent malicious URLs. Remove all HTML tags.

- When designing flows, consider which fields are accessible to your users. Some users may not have access to certain fields, and other users may have access to those fields.

- Flows fail when a filter condition from a Get/Update record element references a null value. Use a decision element to check if the value is null before referencing it in the filter condition.

- Salesforce does not save flow changes automatically. You must explicitly save them often so as not to lose your work.

Take a look at flow limits from the Salesforce site for up-to-date information. As with all other limits in Salesforce, flow limits vary by your user license; you can refer to the official documentation at *Flow Limits and Considerations*: `https://help.salesforce.com/s/articleView?id=sf.flow_considerations.htm&type=5`.

Now that we've reviewed some important flow limits, it's time to summarize this chapter.

Summary

In this chapter, you learned how to use the flow debug feature. You understood a flow interview from start to finish for a good use case, encountering no faults at any steps. This is the first step you need to take to make sure at least one scenario works flawlessly. We learned about various ways of catching flow errors and how we can utilize fault connectors to elements on the screen or send notification emails to your admins. We reviewed what to look for and troubleshooting flows, as well as customized error messages so that your users are informed. We concluded with a practical scenario introducing errors into our flow and seeing the executing steps in the debug details.

In the next chapter, we will explore how we can streamline and enable complex business processes using flow orchestration.

Questions

1. What is a flow interview?

2. What is a fault connector, and how do you add one to your flow elements?

3. What is the best way to find errors in your flow?

Further reading

- *Flow Limits and Considerations*: `https://help.salesforce.com/s/articleView?id=sf.flow_considerations.htm&type=5`

- *Flow Bulkification in Transactions*: `https://help.salesforce.com/s/articleView?id=sf.flow_concepts_bulkification.htm&type=5`

- *Customize What Happens When a Flow Fails*: `https://help.salesforce.com/s/articleView?id=sf.flow_build_logic_fault.htm&type=5`

- *Other Examples of Error Handling in Flows*: `https://help.salesforce.com/s/articleView?language=en_US&id=sf.flow_build_logic_fault_examples.htm&type=5`

Part 3:
Flow Orchestration

In this last part, you will learn to unify complex business processes without code using flow orchestration. Flow orchestration helps you quickly create sophisticated, multi-user, multi-step processes declaratively. You will see how you can amplify the impact of flows.

We will explore and learn important building blocks that we can use to build flow orchestration. We will learn ways to monitor and streamline orchestrations as well as key considerations to make your orchestration effective.

Finally, we will review real-world business scenarios and see how to automate the business processes. You will learn how flow orchestration can bridge gaps in complex business processes.

The following chapters will be covered in this part.

- *Chapter 9, Flow Orchestration*
- *Chapter 10, Compose and Orchestrate Business Processes*

9

Flow Orchestration

So far, we learned the building block of Flow Builder, understood the intricacies of various flow types, and observed the power of Salesforce flows. We gained insight into how to transform and automate business needs into business processes and then create an amazing user experience.

In this chapter, we will explore and see how we can streamline and enable complex business processes using flow orchestration. We will explore and learn flow building blocks and how these blocks work, and then discuss steps to create a flow orchestration. We will explore ways to monitor and streamline our orchestration as well as key considerations to make your orchestration effective.

Flow orchestration helps you to quickly create sophisticated, multi-user, multistep processes declaratively. Due to the low code nature of orchestration, admins can now enable business processes quickly and be able to maintain seamless business workflows. You will see how you can amplify the impact of flows with an orchestrator.

In this chapter, we will cover the following topics:

- What is flow orchestration?
- Orchestration types
- Orchestration – how it works
- Putting it all together to create a model
- Monitoring flow orchestrations
- Debugging orchestration runs

Since flow orchestration is relatively new and new features are added during each release, let's get started with the basics.

What is flow orchestration?

Flow orchestration helps with automating complex multi-user, multi-set processes using Salesforce building task management. You will be able to combine multiple interrelated processes that involve multiple teams into one cohesive integrated streamlined workflow.

With built-in task guidance, team members know exactly what they are supposed to do and at what point — so, essentially, handoffs and approvals are streamlined, making your business process automation more meaningful, effective, and impactful.

With orchestration, we can streamline complex end-to-end business processes:

- **Unify**: Automate multiple workflows in a single end-to-end view
- **Scale**: Be able to create processes quickly with reusable automated actions and components
- **Optimization**: Reduce time between tasks by optimizing notifications and work items and creating user-centric workflows

> **Difference between flows and flow orchestrations**
>
> - A **flow** is an application that automates your business process and makes changes to your data records. They are record-centric, they can do **create, read, update, and delete (CRUD)** operations on your records, and they can span multiple objects.
> - A **flow orchestration** is a user-centric application that can be used to build complex business processes using a series of flows in a coordinated manner. We can enable business processes so that different users can perform business functions seamlessly.

Orchestration types

A flow orchestration has two main types:

- **Autolaunched Orchestration (No Trigger)**: Triggered by Apex, custom buttons, custom URLs, or REST API from third-party systems.
- **Record-Triggered Orchestration**: Triggered when a record is created or updated. We can create a multistep, multi-user process orchestration.

To create a new flow orchestration, follow these steps:

1. Go to **Setup | Process Automation | Flows**.
2. Select **New Flows**.
3. Navigate to the **All + Templates** tab.
4. Select **Flow Orchestration**.

5.   From the canvas, you will be able to create two orchestration types; namely, **Autolaunched Orchestration (No Trigger)** and **Record-Triggered Orchestration**. See *Figure 9.1*:

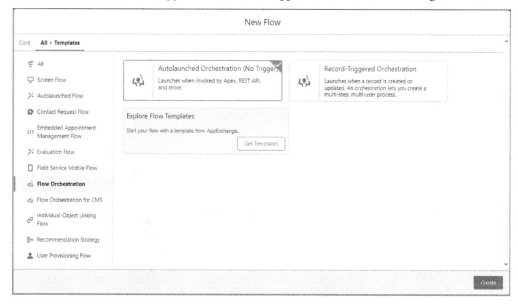

Figure 9.1 – Flow Orchestration creation page

In the next section, let's see how they really work under the hood.

Orchestration – how it works

We use three main building blocks to create a flow orchestration. They are stages, steps, and individual flows. In addition, we optionally have two more building blocks called **Go to Elements** and **Work Guide**. Let's look at and see how these building blocks work:

- **Stage**: A group of steps, organized logically, that run sequentially. These steps in the stages can run interactively or in the background. Only one stage can run at any point in the orchestration. An orchestration must contain at least one stage.

- **Step**: These are workflows/automated processes that can run sequentially or concurrently within a stage. Each step is a flow and, as we already know, flows can be run interactively or in the background.

- **Flows**: Steps require a flow to run an orchestration. An interactive step runs a screen flow. A background step runs an autolaunched flow.

- **Go to Elements**: Connectors for routing to stages.

- **Trigger**: Just as with flows, an action or event will trigger an orchestration run. When we build the orchestration, you can specify the triggering mechanism for flows.

Orchestration is launched via an autolaunched or record-triggered orchestration, and this is the start icon on our canvas. Then, we have the first stage, and each stage will contain a set of steps that can run sequentially and/or concurrently. See *Figure 9.2*; here, we have **Stage-1** with one interactive step (*example*: screen flow for the user to input data) and a background step (*example*: send notification).

We then have a **Decision** element; based on a specific decision, we can divert the orchestration to take a specific path.

Then, we have the second stage and a set of steps related to this stage. **Stage2_Step1** is a data input screen flow (*example*: data input for different users), and **Step2** is the background step (*example*: creating a case).

Based on the complexity of your business process, you can have multiple stages and steps within each stage. At any point in the orchestration run, only one stage can run. Refer to *Figure 9.2* to get an idea of how a flow orchestration looks:

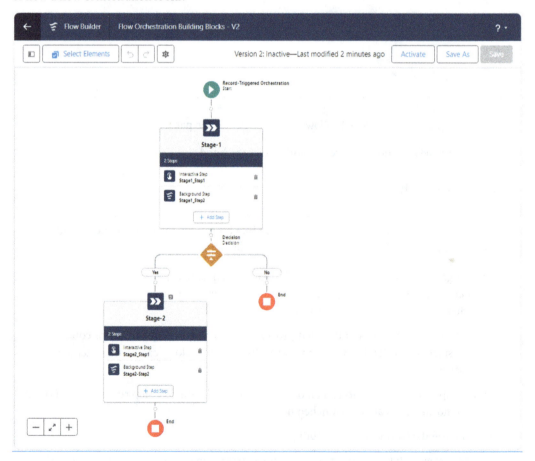

Figure 9.2 – Flow building blocks

So far, we have seen activities related to building flow orchestration, and these are activities performed by your admin or technical team members. Next, we will see how and where your users interact with orchestration.

Work Guide

Orchestration lets us personalize tasks and action items so that business users can view and complete their tasks on each record page. This is required when you want users to interact on the screen. When there are interaction steps in the orchestration, it will create a work item and assign it to a user, queue, or group as defined in the orchestration. Users will be able to complete work items from the orchestration work guide available on the Salesforce Lightning record page. See *Figure 9.3*.

You can add the Work Guide from **App Launcher | Object** (in our case, **Account**) **| Lightning Record Pages**.

Go to the **Account** page(s) and add the **Flow Orchestration Work Guide** component to the Lightning page (drag and drop).

Visit the *Lightning App Builder | Salesforce Trailhead* web page to learn about Lightning App Builder: https://trailhead.salesforce.com/content/learn/modules/lightning_ app_builder:

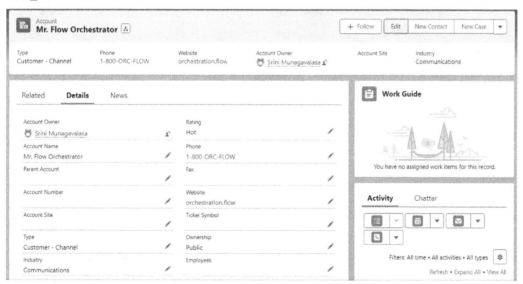

Figure 9.3 – Work Guide on the Lightning record page

In the next sections, let's put all the orchestration Lego blocks together to create a model.

Putting it all together to create a model

Flow orchestrations, as we know, are very complex and get very complicated. As we did for flows, we need to define business process flows and the entire orchestration flow. We need to map out each of the individual processes' flows and understand the relationships between them. We will review real-life scenarios in the next chapter and create a flow orchestration so that you can understand the concepts.

We will check and see the detailed steps around creating flow orchestration. We will see each task in more detail, which is needed to create a record-triggered orchestration. Let's assume that we created all the required flows for our orchestration:

1. Click on new flow orchestration from **New Flow | All + Templates**.

2. Start **Record-Triggered Orchestration** by configuring the following options:

    A. **Select Object**: Select whose records trigger the orchestration.

    B. **Configure Trigger**: Trigger the orchestration when 1) a record is created, 2) a record is updated, or 3) a record is created or updated.

    C. **Set Entry Conditions**: To minimize unwanted orchestration executions:

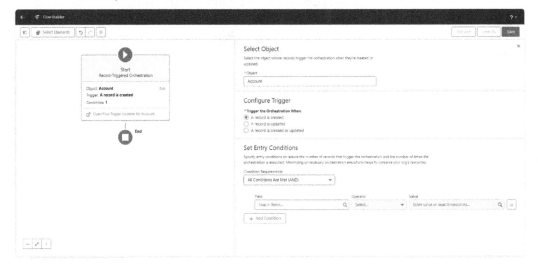

Figure 9.4 – New flow orchestration: Starting Record-Triggered Orchestration

3. Hover over the circle between the **Start** and **End** elements. Click on the + symbol to add an element – a **Stage** element or a **Decision** element.

4. Under **Add Element**, click on **Stage** to add a new stage and add the following (see *Figure 9.5*):

    A. Label

    B. API name

    C.   Description

    D.   A condition for when to complete the stage:

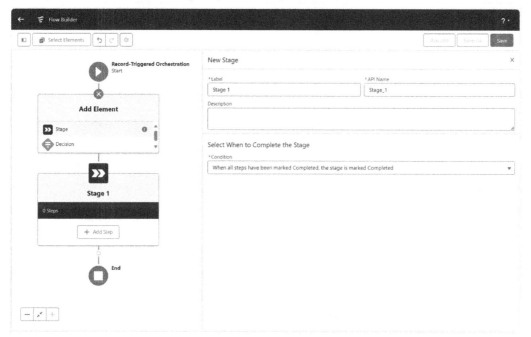

Figure 9.5 – Adding a New Stage flow orchestration

5.   For each of these stages, we need to add steps. Steps in a stage can run sequentially or parallelly.

6.   Click on **+ Add Step** and pick one of the three available steps – **Interactive Step**, **Background Step**, or **MuleSoft Step** (see *Figure 9.6*).

7.   **Interactive Step**: These steps are interactive, and the user performs this action. We can configure the interactive step by doing the following (see *Figure 9.6*):

    I.   Select a condition to start the step.

    II.   **Action**: We need an active screen flow to run when the step starts (as discussed, these flows need to be created, tested, and activated so that we can use them during the orchestration step).

    III. **Assignee Type** and **User** resources: Someone who completes this action. This can be a user, group, or queue and can be static value or dynamic.

    IV. **Select Where to Complete the Action**: Enter the ID of the related record that has a page layout with the **Flow Orchestration Work Guide** component on it. This is where the assignee completes their assigned work.

V.   Specify a condition for when to complete the step:

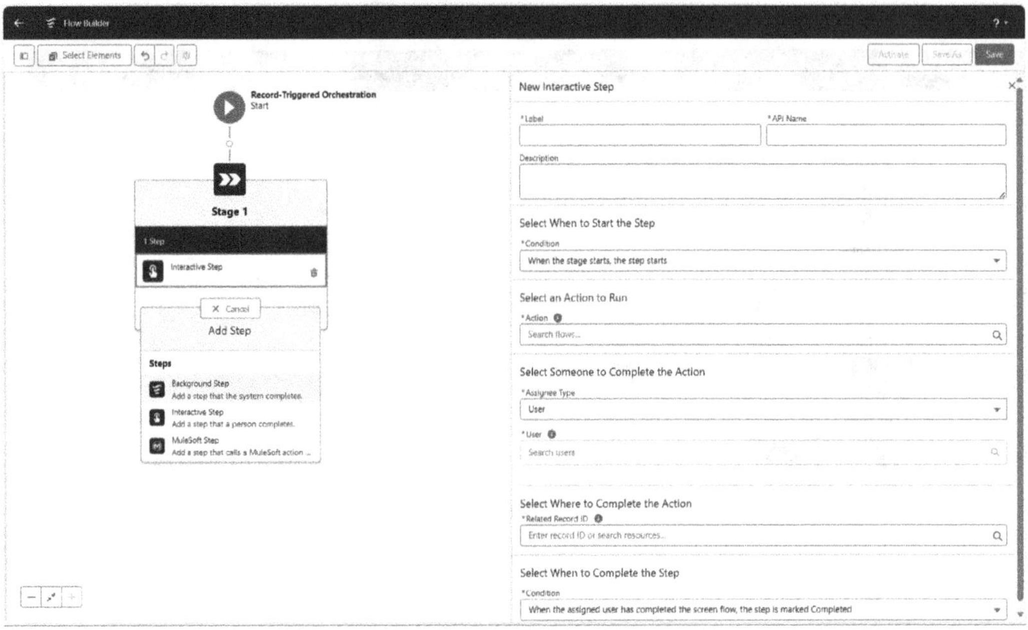

Figure 9.6 – Adding a step to a flow orchestration: Interactive Step using screen flow

8. **Background Step**: The system performs this action in the background:

I.   Select a condition to start the step.

II.   If this is not the first step, choose another step in the same stage to wait for completion before starting this step.

III. **Select an Action to Run**: Select an autolaunched flow to run when the step starts. (As discussed, these flows need to be created, tested, and activated).

9. **MuleSoft Step**: The MuleSoft step runs an operation imported from a MuleSoft API and has no user interaction. They run asynchronously:

I.   Select a condition to start the step.

II.   Select a MuleSoft action to run when the step starts:

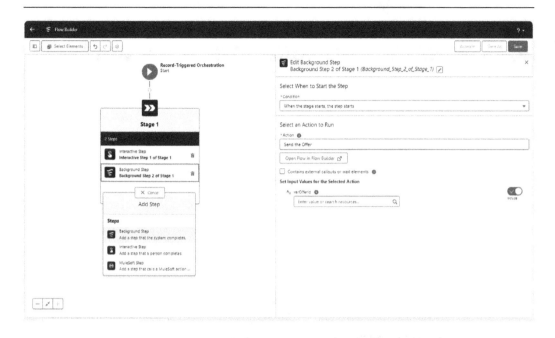

Figure 9.7 – Adding a step to a flow orchestration: Background Step

As we can see, you can add multiple steps to a stage. Only one stage can run during flow orchestration, but steps can run sequentially or concurrently.

One more important building block I would like to highlight here is our **Decision** element. Any business process has many decision-making points, and so do our flows and flow orchestrations. Just as with flows, this decision flow element evaluates outcomes starting from the top and executes the first one whose conditions are met. See *Figure 9.8*.

We can use **Decision** elements and separate stages to support complex business logic:

Figure 9.8 – Adding a Decision element to a flow orchestration

10. Save and activate a flow orchestration. You will be prompted to give a name to the flow orchestration.

Let's see which features we have to monitor our flow orchestrations.

Monitoring flow orchestrations

We can monitor and streamline the orchestrations that we have configured. With this feature, we will be able to identify bottlenecks and opportunities and enhance the performance of individual executions of the orchestration stage and steps.

You run the flow orchestration from the object that you defined. For record-triggered orchestrations, create a record for the object or make an update to the record to trigger the flow orchestration. This action creates a work item and is available in the **Orchestration Work Guide** on the **Lightning record** page.

Users will see these work tasks in the work guide, and they will be able to perform them. For instance, more work tasks will be created and assigned to the same user or different users or groups for a given flow orchestration based on input from the prior screen and decision elements in the orchestration. In addition, your admin or your tech team members will be able to monitor flow orchestrations by accessing objects— orchestration items and orchestration runs.

Flow Orchestration Work Guide is a screen component. You can add this to a record page via App Builder. During the orchestration run, any interactive step will generate a work item for the user.

Users are notified with a link and will be able to access and complete their tasks in the work guide available on the record page.

When a task is assigned, it shows up on the record page for the user. In *Figure 9.9A*, the flow orchestration assigns a work task, requesting the user to complete the work. Our flow orchestration waits for the user input, continues with the run after the user input value, and clicks on **Next** in the screen component:

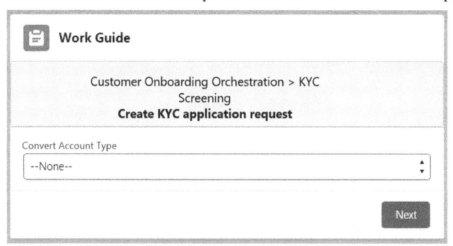

Figure 9.9A – Work Guide task assigned to the user by flow orchestration run

If there are more items, the same will be notified to the user. If there are approval steps or tasks requiring input from another user, an approval task may be assigned to that user(s). See *Figure 9.9B*:

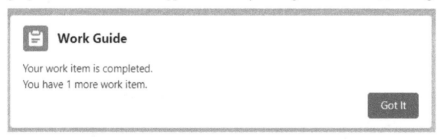

Figure 9.9B – Work Guide notifying users that there are more future tasks

After all the work tasks are completed, the **Work Guide** component on the record page displays the message, as shown in *Figure 9.9C*, that there are no assigned work items for this record:

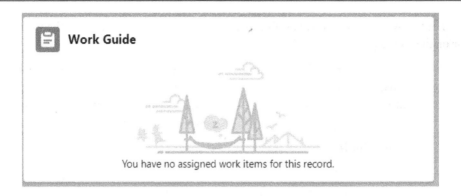

Figure 9.9C – Work Guide message

In addition to user-assigned work tasks, your user as well as your admin will be able to view work items from the **Orchestration Work Items** object. You can create a list view based on stage, just as with any other list view control. See *Figure 9.10*. You can navigate to the work items by clicking on the context record to open the **Work Guide** section on the record page. See *Figure 9.3* for the **Work Guide** section, on the right side of the page layout. If work items are assigned, the user will see those items here. We will discuss this end-to-end process in the next chapter:

Figure 9.10 - List view control of my work items

The **Orchestration Runs** object will display all orchestrations with the status of the run. See *Figure 9.11*:

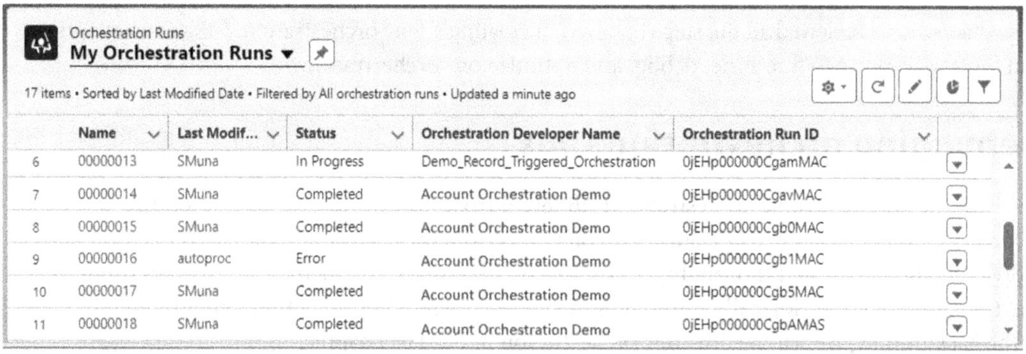

Figure 9.11 – Orchestration Runs list view control

To find details about each orchestration run, simply click on the **Name** record; this will open the details page, as shown in *Figure 9.12*. It will give the status of every stage and step in the orchestration run, as well as when it started, ended, or failed:

Figure 9.12 – Orchestration Run: detailed status of the run

Now that we have reviewed all the steps involved in creating a flow orchestration, let's see what options and tools we can use to fine-tune, debug, and optimize our orchestration.

Debugging orchestration runs

The debug function for flow orchestration is different from flow debug; we will review this in a later section. We do not have a debug feature to debug flows from orchestration, so we need to ensure those individual flows are tested thoroughly. Via a flow orchestration, we lined up these flows using steps and then grouped steps logically into stages. A stage is triggered by an action either interactively or in the background. We will see the flow orchestration in our last chapter.

Ensure that all the flows you plan to use in flow orchestrations are thoroughly tested and optimized. During orchestration debugging, the Flow Builder tool for orchestration will provide what steps failed at what stage. Since flows are used in orchestration steps, it is critical that flows are tested and ready to use.

We can debug orchestrations when they are in progress. Essentially, any user interaction orchestration flow can be debugged. This feature will help us better understand different scenarios and the paths our orchestration runs take and gain insight into how they work.

From the orchestration run list view, admins can cancel an orchestration or be able to debug an orchestration. See *Figure 9.13A*. You have this option only for orchestration runs with **Status** = **In Progress**:

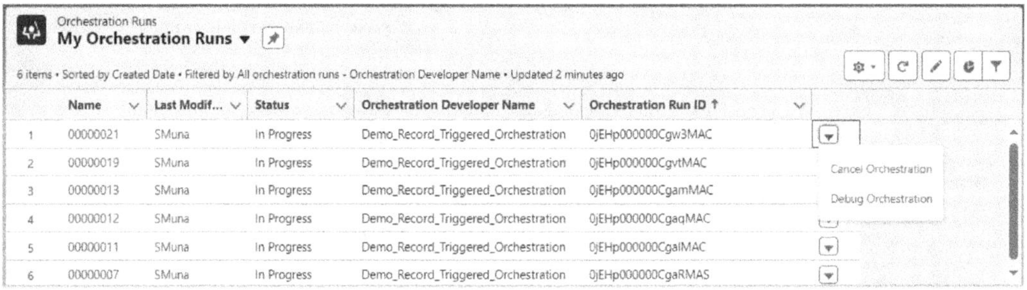

Figure 9.13A – Orchestration Runs (option to cancel or debug)

Click on **Debug Orchestration** from the last column of the record to open the orchestration run in the debug window. The failed path is highlighted with a thicker line (I added a yellow-colored line so that it can be seen clearly), and in the right pane, you can see **Debug Details**. Failed stages, steps, and decisions are shown in thicker lines. You will know exactly where it failed so that you can fix a specific flow in the step or the decision element. Most of the time, it will be the flow that fails, and you will be able to test the individual flow and fix the underlying issue. The orchestration run fails at the first error it encounters. So, if you have more issues down the line, fix the first one and continue re-testing along the path. In *Figure 9.13B*, we can clearly see some steps in **Stage-2** failed:

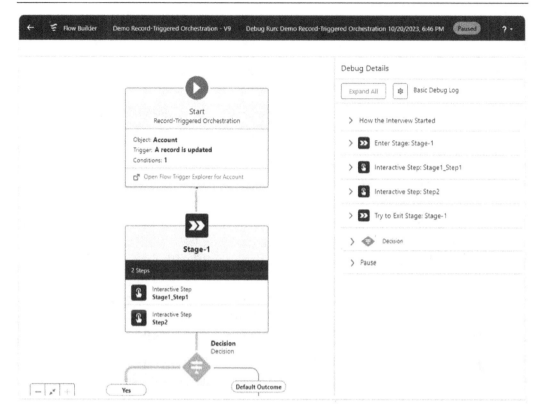

Figure 9.13B – Orchestration runs: debug screen

Building a flow orchestration is relatively simple. The most difficult part is planning and designing how you want to articulate your business processes from a user-role perspective. If you and your team can explain the complete process in simple terms, flow orchestration is the way to go. As with flows, flow orchestrations are visual, and you have a great tool to monitor them. All you need now is some practice. Go to your development sandbox and start creating some hypothetical scenarios and testing them out.

Let's look at some key considerations that can help you avoid running into issues with your orchestration.

Key considerations when orchestrating flows

You need flows to create flow orchestrations, but you also need to plan for the orchestration and then design and develop the right flow. This means we need to take our flow orchestration into account, at least in the solution design phase of our project. Consider the following points:

- When do we start our business process, and when do we end it? We need to explore and analyze all possible process paths and pick the one that best fits our business needs.

- How are we assigning tasks to roles? We do not assign users to tasks; rather, we assign tasks to roles and then roles to users or groups.

- Identify entry conditions and fine-tune them to optimize your process. Eliminate redundancies as much as possible.

- Check to see all your existing flows and see whether you can use them in flow orchestration.

- Do not start building your orchestration unless your business process is finalized, understood, and agreed upon by all your project stakeholders.

- Most flows can be developed with click and low code, but orchestrations need some level of coding skills. Make sure to involve technical SMEs to review your flow orchestrations.

- Also, during CRP sessions, it will be very helpful for you and the team if your orchestrations can be demonstrated to key stakeholders and project team members. It will be beneficial for you to do internal demos with the core project team and get feedback to optimize the stages and steps in your flow.

- Do not just create flow orchestrations for the sake of it. Even complex business processes can be developed using flows. You have more control over your flows as you test and debug them from end to end. At this time, flow orchestrations cannot be debugged like you do for flows.

- Design flows in orchestration to avoid data input failures.

- Background orchestrations do not pause; to debug them, add interactive steps (just for testing) so that you can inspect the flow and values.

You need to identify, analyze, design, develop, and test all the individual flows that you need for your flow orchestration. All you orchestrate is bringing all these flows logically together so as to produce a smooth flow for your users and get the maximum effect on your business processes. With this, let's summarize this chapter.

Summary

In this chapter, you learned how flow orchestration helps us to quickly create sophisticated, multi-user, multistep processes declaratively. We can build end-to-end complex business processes in one single functional module using flow orchestration and amplify the impact of flows. We use simple building blocks called stages and steps that help group flow and create highly interactive workflow actions that can be managed and completed by cross-department business users or groups. We also touched upon features to monitor and streamline our orchestration.

In the last chapter, we will explore and discuss a few complex business scenarios and walk through a complex business process orchestration. We will see business use cases, create a business process flow, identify individual flows, and then automate the process using flow orchestration.

Questions

1. Define flow orchestration stages and steps.

2. Where do your users see orchestration work tasks?

3. What are the main types of flow orchestrations?

4. What is a Work Guide?

5. How can I as an admin find out the status of my orchestration run?

Further reading

- Salesforce flow orchestration documentation: `https://help.salesforce.com/s/articleView?id=sf.orchestrator_flow_orchestrator.htm&type=5`

- Salesforce Trailhead – *Flow Orchestration Basics*: `https://trailhead.salesforce.com/content/learn/modules/orchestrator-basics`

- Salesforce Trailhead – *Orchestrate Complex Processes with Flow Orchestration*: `https://trailhead.salesforce.com/content/learn/modules/build-a-flow-orchestration`

10
Compose and Orchestrate Business Processes

In the last chapter, we discussed in detail how to streamline and enable complex business processes using flow orchestration. We explored and learned flow building blocks, saw how they work, and then discussed steps to create a flow orchestration. We also reviewed ways to monitor and streamline our orchestration.

In this last chapter, we will look at a practical scenario, a simplified real-world business requirement, a business process flow, and finally, a flow orchestration that meets our business needs. Also, we will look at how we keep an eye on making our orchestration efficient, effective, simple, and usable.

We will cover the following topics:

- Real-world business scenarios
- Designing and creating a business process flow diagram
- Transforming business processes into automated solutions
- Tips and tricks

First, let us look at real-world complex business scenarios (a simplified version) and understand business process flow from start to finish.

Real-world business scenarios

In this section, we will look at two scenarios and review business process flows. We will look at the conceptual and detailed business process flow for partner registration and quote approvals. Of the two scenarios, we will walk through the orchestration process from start to finish for the quote approval scenario.

Scenario 1 – a partner registration business process

Partner registration is an end-to-end process, involving registering and onboarding your channel partners so that they can be part of the partner program. Partner users will be able to access your system and collaborate with internal team members of your business.

Our scenario is to enable the channel team to capture data from partner users and be able to complete onboarding activities – request account, contact, and user creation – so that partners can access Salesforce data and collaborate and work with the sales team in generation and closing deals.

Let us break this down into digestible steps:

The business process starts with the partner user requesting access and being able to get access to the Salesforce system, enabling them to access an account and related information such as contacts, opportunities, cases, marketing development funds, and campaigns.

1. Your partner (channel partner) requests registration to your **Partner Relationship Management (PRM)** system to access customer data and do so collaboratively with your sales team.

2. The channel team receives a registration request from partners via manual email or over the phone. We can also capture data from channel partner users directly via Experience Cloud, but we will leave this out intentionally to simplify the process.

3. The channel team reviews and confirms partner requests.

4. Request sales operations to create accounts and a contact record.

5. The sales ops creates accounts and contact records and adds account team members as needed, in consultation with the account manager.

6. Sales ops requests Sys Admins to create/activate partner users.

7. On creation, the partner user is notified that they can now access the system, with detailed steps provided and who to contact with any questions/concerns.

8. The process ends when a partner user record is successfully created.

A simplified process flow diagram of this process is shown in *Figure 10.1*.

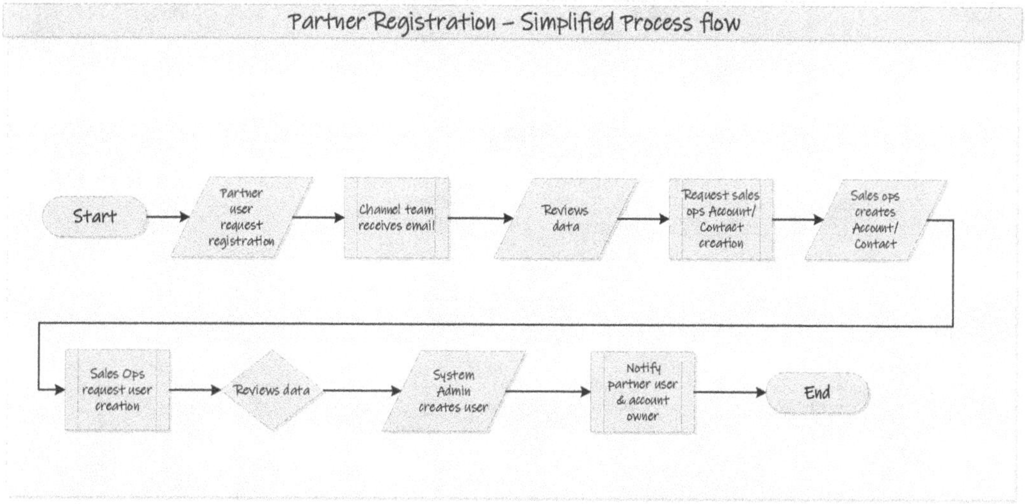

Figure 10.1 – Partner registration - Simplified Process Flow

We will take this conceptual process flow, refine it, and capture more granular details later in this chapter. Let us look at our next scenario for quote approval.

Scenario 2 – a quote approval business process

This process is for a large corporation where the opportunity/quote process is highly complex. Also, there are certain prerequisites, such as quotes, that can only be generated after KYC and risk analysis is completed and the prospect is converted to a customer. We will not go into detail; we will simply simplify the business process so that you understand the basic concepts.

The following are the high-level steps from our scenario (as shown in *Figure 10.2*):

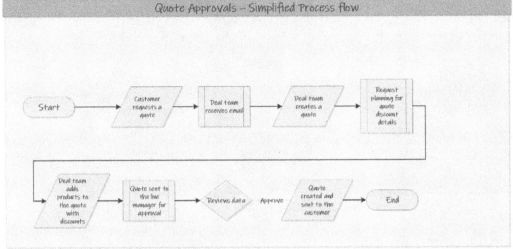

Figure 10.2 – Quote approvals – a simplified process flow

1. Your customer requests a quote.

2. The deal team gets notified with the quote details.

3. The deal team validates prerequisites and creates a quote.

4. The planning team is notified; discount details are added as per the account entitlements.

5. Approval notification is sent to the line manager. There will be multiple levels of approval, based on attributes such as account type, product family, and industry.

6. Upon approval, the quotes are created successfully with the right discounts.

7. The customer is notified with the quote details, the next steps to take, and a copy of the quote.

These process flows are your first steps during the plan and design phase of the project. They are simple and easy to follow for all project stakeholders. Then, consider some questions. Where does the process start, what are the high-level steps (do not try to solve this during this phase), and how does that end? Take notes while discussing and getting agreement during your workshops or **Conference Room Pilots (CRPs)** with key project stakeholders. That will be helpful in the next phase of the project, and we will see how these simple process flows are transformed into more detailed future state business process flows in the next section. Note that the process flow we discussed here is a simplified version so that I can explain to you the concepts and essence of flow orchestration. I have worked on complex quote process automation, and it is very complex, and integration and automation span multiple systems such as Salesforce, CPQ, and SAP.

Designing and creating a business process flow diagram

Let's take our simplified flow and see how it is transformed into detailed process steps. These business process flows not only help everyone on the project team understand the business needs but also help us identify what parts of these process steps can, and should, be automated. A good business process flow is a key success factor for any flow orchestration.

A partner registration scenario

In this scenario, your project team needs to create these business process flow diagrams irrespective of automation or manual steps. For the most part, based on my experience, we should start small and automate only key steps, focusing on implementing functionality so that your business users can use a tool, module, or system.

It's always beneficial to add automation iteratively and incrementally.

Let's go a few layers deep and see how we can refine the initial business process flows we created in the prior section.

Let's identify what steps in the business process flow can be automated (as shown in *Figure 10.3*):

A. A partner (channel partner) requests registration.

B. The channel team receives a registration request from the partners. This is our screen flow (*step 1* – see Partner Registration Process Flow).

C. The channel team reviews and confirms partner requests. This can also be done as part of *step 1*.

D. Request sales operations to create accounts and a contact record (this is *step 2*).

E. Sales ops creates accounts and contact records and adds account team members (*steps 3 and 4*). We can automate account and contact creation in these steps.

F. Sales ops requests that Sys Admins create or activate partner users. *Step 5* is partially automated in our scenario, where we automatically create a user, but the system administrator validates and adds the right role or profile to the user.

G. On creation, the partner user is notified (*step 6*).

H. Optionally, we can notify the channel team and account owner (*step 7*).

This enhanced future state after a few iterations looks like *Figure 10.3*. This process flow becomes your current "as-is" after implementing the functionality. A **business process flow** is a snapshot of your business process at a point in time. So, as we start adding functionality and automation in future iterations, we keep updating this process flow and make a future process flow.

Look at the transformation from *Figure 10.1* to *Figure 10.3*. To understand concepts and examples of business process flow, you can refer to *Chapter 4* of my book *The Salesforce Business Analyst*.

In the following figure, we have added swim lanes to identify who (i.e., which persona) is responsible for the steps. We have created a detailed business process flow, step by step, capturing our business needs.

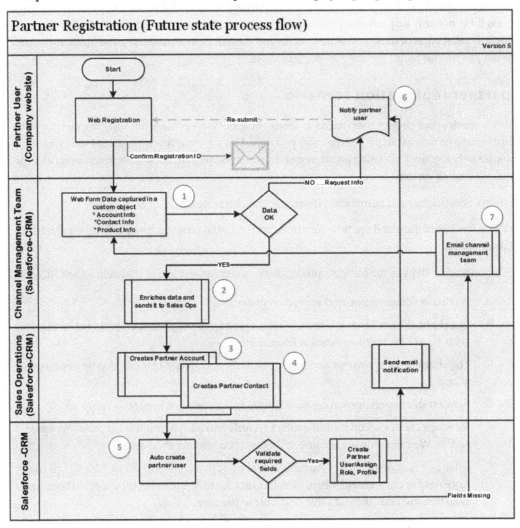

Figure 10.3 – Partner registration – a future state process flow

Let us look at and see what a detailed future state looks like in *scenario 2*.

The quote approvals scenario

Like *scenario 1*, as we run this process with key stakeholders, we can find gaps as well as opportunities that we can capture and add to the business process flow. A business process flow is not just limited to a project or a release. We need to create a business process flow or the entire life cycle of the business and keep it alive by keeping it current and relevant.

The following flow is self-explanatory and highly simplified. We will be able to fulfill this requirement just with flows too. This example scenario depicts using the approval process with flows and building a complete quote management functionality. Use the following business process flow to build your flow orchestration.

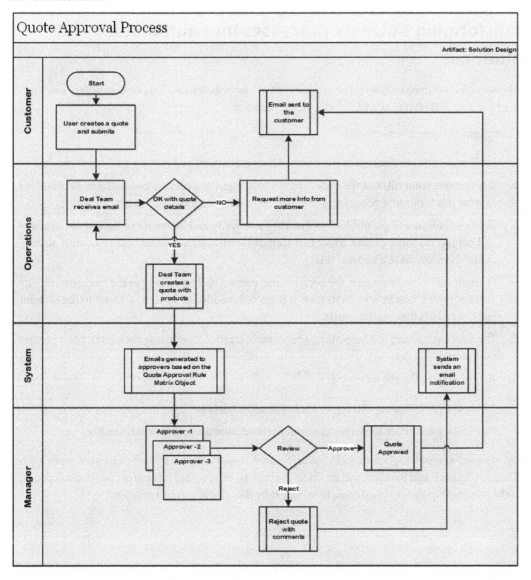

Figure 10.4 – The quote approval process

So far, we have seen how we can develop a business process flow step by step, from start to finish. For all project team members and key stakeholders to understand what they are trying to accomplish as part of a project, they should understand the business processes and business requirements. Enabling functionality comes before any automation, and we, the project team, should logically group functionality with automation, prioritizing what makes sense to our business.

In the next section, let us look at flow orchestration for one of the preceding scenarios.

Transforming business processes into automated solutions

In this section, let's explore flow orchestration for partner registration. This is an excellent example, as we have screen elements as well as backend automation.

Let's implement a simplified scenario:

1. Flow orchestration runs when the parent account is active, and partner enabled is checked.

2. The channel team fills out the onboarding form, inputting contact and account details. Let's assume this is our first release and the channel team will input the data accurately.

3. Sales operations will get notified so that they can verify and authorize or decline the account and contact creation. (Think about this scenario – what if an account and/or contact already exists? How would you address this?)

4. On approval from Salesforce, the account and contact will be created in the background. The account from where flow orchestration is triggered is added as a parent account to the account just created via flow orchestration.

5. The Salesforce admin will be notified after contact creation, converting the contract to a partner user record.

6. An email is sent to the following:

   I.   The partner user with registration and access details

   II. The partner account manager with account, contact, and user information

Here, I created a record-triggered orchestration on an Account object. All types of account types, such as Direct, Channel, and Reseller, will sit under a child account under one parent portfolio account, and the relationship with the customer is managed by this global account manager.

I have simplified the process here and created three stages (stage 1, stage 2, and stage 3). With flow orchestration, it is one big auto-layout (there is no free-form option available at the time of writing this book; I am sure this option will be released in a future release). I have had to remove many steps within the stages to accommodate and make the flow orchestration cleaner (see *Figure 10.5A* and *Figure 10.5B*):

- **Stage 1**: Capture partner info:

  - **Step 1**: Account info – Capture the partner account and contact-related info.

  - **Step 2**: Notify sales ops.

We have a manual step where Sales Ops completes the rest of the information as needed and works with account managers. A flag is updated on the Account record if this partner request is approved or rejected.

We have a decision element where we check the account owner's decision from the Account record:

- **Stage 2**: Create a partner account and contact:

  - **Step 1**: Create a partner account.

  - **Step 2**: Create a partner contact.

    - **Step 2.1**: Additionally, you can send a notification to the sales ops and channel teams (not shown in the following figures).

  - **Step 3**: This is an interactive step where channel manager approval criteria are captured.

The decision element is where the channel manager approves or declines the account.

If declined, this flow goes back to *stage 2*, and we can add additional steps to validate the process:

- **Stage 3**: Create Partner User:

  - **Step 1**: Create a partner user.

  - **Step 2**: Notify the account owner and account team.

  - **Step 3**: Notify the partner user.

As discussed in *Chapter 9*, to create a new orchestration, click on a new flow orchestration from **New Flow | All + Templates** and select **Start Record-Triggered Orchestration**:

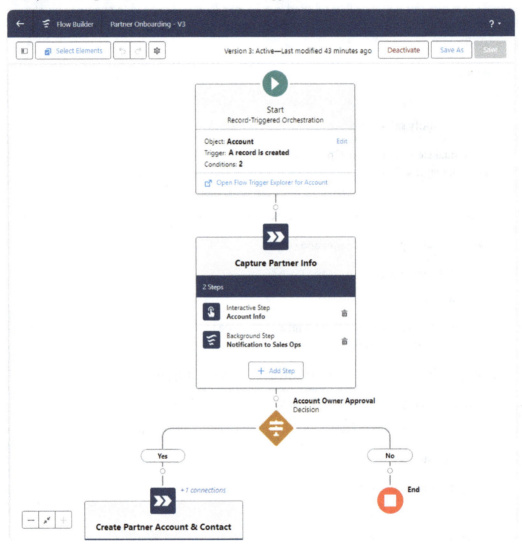

Figure 10.5A – Partner onboarding – flow orchestration

Figure 10.5B is a continuation of *Figure 10.5A*:

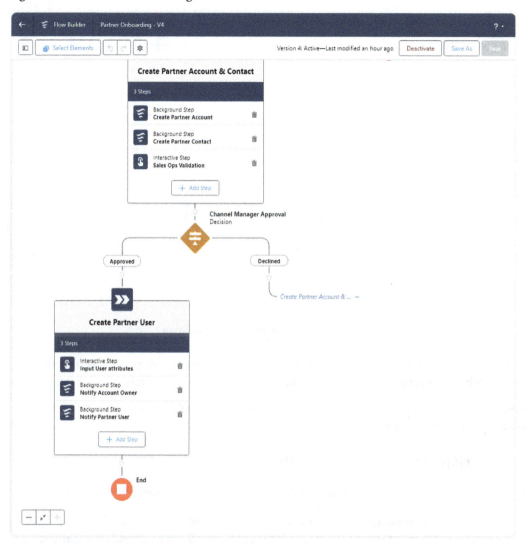

Figure 10.5B – Partner onboarding – flow orchestration (continued)

When account team members create or update an account, and if the account type is active, the channel selling flag is marked approved, our flow orchestration runs and orchestration work items are created and assigned to users, as defined in the flow orchestration steps.

Figure 10.6 shows the work guide assigned to a user on the **Account** screen.

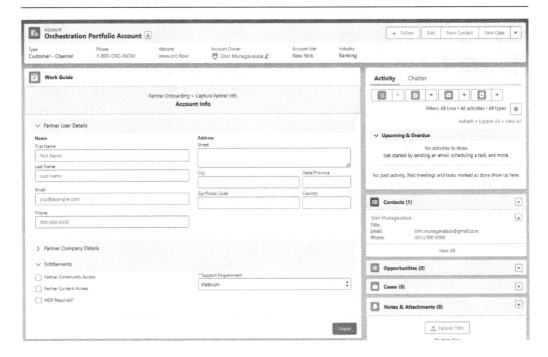

Figure 10.6 – The flow orchestration work guide

Responsible team members are notified via email and can also access work guide tasks from the list view. Step-by-step instructions on how to create a flow orchestration were featured in *Chapter 9*.

Now, you can see how easy it is for us to create flow orchestration if we have a good understanding of the business process flows.

Key considerations during flows

Let's look at some key considerations that can help you avoid running into issues with your orchestration:

- You, the project team, and business stakeholders should understand the business "as-is" and "to-be" processes from start to finish. Take time to plan in creating and getting a common understanding.

- Just because you need to create a flow for your flow orchestration, do not create redundant flows. Reuse an existing flow. If needed, adjust it to fit your needs.

- User proper naming conventions, and document where possible for every flow, stage, step, and so on. When implementing flow orchestrations, it would be beneficial to provide a link to your KB articles (including BRD, process flows, etc.). The best location to add documentation and all relevant links is in the description field when you save your orchestration.

- Do not complicate orchestrations by adding too many features; add what is needed by your users to have a great user experience, even if it means implementing simpler automation initially.

- Your work is not done after you deploy your orchestration. You need to plan to iteratively improve and optimize, as new features emerge and business processes change all the time.

- When you debug a flow or flow orchestration, it confines you to what is within the flow. However, flow behaves differently in real-world scenarios. Debugging is very helpful to see how your process works and helps with fine-tuning, but it does not replace testing. Make sure to test the flow in a sandbox to test real-world scenarios and edge cases.

- Use the same discipline as you do for any of your development work. Use the development box to create your orchestration and flow, and then test your units. Transfer them to SIT for quality assurance testing, UAT for usability testing, and then, using your preferred migration tool, transfer your work to production following UAT clearance. Whether it's code, low-code, or no-code, you have to follow the right process.

- Lastly, I want to emphasize again – plan what flow you need for your organization. Make sure it is tested and fine-tuned before you use it in your orchestration.

Let's conclude this last section and summarize what we learned in this chapter.

Summary

In this chapter, you got a good glimpse of how to orchestrate your business processes using flows. Flow orchestration, like any other tool when used wisely, can add immense benefit to your business user. Flow by itself performs much more complex automation, where it can simplify the tasks performed by your business users, remove redundancies, and maintain high-quality data in a system. Flow orchestration goes above and beyond, by notifying and creating work items only when you need your business users to take some action. Orchestrations are not just for complex business processes; you can use them even for simple business processes to streamline and create meaningful workflows. Flow orchestration is relatively new, and we will see many new features and functions in the future.

We have reached the end of this book. Thank you for taking the time to explore business process automation using flows with me. Start with drawing the process flows, even if you must draw them on a paper napkin before you design Salesforce flows. Keep practicing, and start implementing flows and flow orchestrations. To keep them current, relevant, and effective, revisit your flows, and keep revisiting and refining your business processes and flow orchestrations. Salesforce flows and flow orchestrations are just getting started. They will be your powerful tool to enable business process automation.

Further reading

Flow Orchestration Limits and Considerations: `https://help.salesforce.com/s/articleView?id=sf.orchestrator_considerations.htm&type=5`

Assessments

Chapter 1, Process Flows – Understanding Business Requirements

1. Process flow helps us capture the business process steps from start to finish. The current state of the process is called "as-is." From "as-is," we will gather requirements and create the future state "to-be" business process flow.

2. Yes. Without understanding business requirements, the team will not be able to design, build, and enable the right product. This will result in a bad final product that will not meet the business's needs.

3. BPMN, Visio, Wrike, lucid chart, and even paper and pen.

4. The RACI matrix helps the project team clarify employee roles and responsibilities for tasks/deliverables on a project. RACI helps with better decision-making. It is also called **RAM**, which stands for **Responsible Assignment Matrix**.

Chapter 2, Identification of Functional Requirements for Automation

1. The steps that can be automated in the prioritized requirements are done during conference room pilots/workshops with project stakeholders, SMEs, and project team members.

2. BPA is to automate repeatable and complex business process steps using software technology.

3. Before you answer this, think of the pain points your users had to go through in your system. Now, think of repetitive steps that you automated. An example would be sending reminders to close the opportunity when the opportunity closing date is in 2 weeks and then 1 week; if no action is taken, send an escalation notice to the manager.

Chapter 3, Business Process Features to Automate

1. Flow charts, BPMN, UML, data flow diagrams, Six Sigma, and TQM.

2. Microsoft Visio, Lucid chart, and flip charts.

3. Validation rules, formulae fields, dependent picklists, workflow approvals, flows, and so on.

Chapter 4, Flow Building Blocks, Triggering, and Entry Conditions

1. An autolaunch flow can be triggered only by a record change, schedule, or platform event.

2. Autolaunch flow does need a trigger within the flow and runs in the background, whereas **Autolaunch flow (no trigger)** has no trigger defined within the flow. They are initiated by something else such as a custom button based on user judgment.

3. Yes and no. Yes, only if your custom button calls a screen flow.

4. When you click on **Actions**, they can call only screen flows, whereas the custom button may not call screens.

Chapter 5, Salesforce Order of Execution

1. The case assignment rule wins. As we saw in the *Salesforce platform Order Of Execution (OOE)* section, *Step 9* runs after *Step 3* and this value shall be overwritten:

   - *Step 3* executes before-save, record-triggered flows

   - *Step 9* executes assignment rules

2. Yes, for the most part, we can control flow execution. Salesforce Flow automation runs in the following order:

   I.   Flows with the same trigger with values from 1 to 1,000 run in ascending order.

   II. Flows with the same trigger order value run in alphabetical order based on the flows' API names.

   III. Flows that are unordered run next based on created dates.

   IV. Flows with trigger order values from 1,001 to 2,000 run next and in ascending order.

3. Learning this order ensures data consistency and helps avoid unexpected issues. When multiple automations such as workflows, assignment rules, escalation rules, and triggers are in place, it is crucial to know the sequence in which Salesforce processes these automations.

4. The OOE for this parent record runs from *Step 1*, so the whole process runs from start to finish for the parent record.

Chapter 6, Types of Salesforce Flows

1. At the time of writing this book, there are five flow types:

    I.   **Screen Flow**: Guides users through a business process interactively.

    II. **Record-Triggered Flow**: Triggered by DML actions such as record create, update, or delete.

    III. **Schedule-Triggered Flow**: Launches at a specified time and frequency.

    IV. **Platform Event—Triggered Flow**: Launches when a platform event message is received.

    V.   **Autolaunched Flow (No Trigger)**: Does not have a trigger defined within the flow. It is triggered on demand as needed.

2. A record-triggered flow is triggered by DML actions such as record creation, update, or deletion.

    So, wanting an action such as sending emails, chatter posts, or updating related records would make a good use case for this type of flow.

3. You can create a list view as shown in *Figure 6.19*:

    Process Type + Trigger = Flow Type

    For **Autolaunched Flow (No Trigger)**, the **Trigger** field is blank.

    Also, remember they are triggered by clicking on a custom button or custom link.

4. We use an after-save trigger when we would like to send a notification or do some action on objects or something that is not the object that triggered. For example, when we want to send an email, update the roll-up summary field, and so on.

5. The Lightning utility bar. By adding a flow component to the app's utility bar, your users will be able to access the flow from any page.

6. We can make flows accessible from the following:

    *   Lightning pages

    *   Custom buttons

    *   Custom links

    *   Lightning utility bar

    *   Flow actions

    *   Visualforce pages

    *   Web tabs

    *   The Experience Builder page

    *   Custom Lightning components

Chapter 7, Flows Using Apex Sharing

1. Flow lets you share records with clicks. The only other way we can access Shared Objects is via Apex Sharing Reason and they are now available from Flow Builder.

2. Apex Sharing Reason helps us identify how a record is shared. This value is assigned to RowCause on the shared object.

3. We can use the delete elements for the object using the flow, and also, delete based on conditions. If the record is shared with multiple users, and you want to delete just one user, make sure you use conditions.

Chapter 8, Optimizing and Troubleshooting Flows

1. A flow interview is a running instance of a flow. A flow is an application that asks you for input and does something in Salesforce based on that input.

2. Configure the fault connectors in your flow so that you always receive an email when a flow fails. Create a case or send flow error notifications to the support team. We can do this by creating a text template and including the values of all flow resources. This will help us see the values the user entered on screen flows and, for other auto-launched flows, the exact value of flow variables in case the interview fails.

3. Test as many scenarios as you can think of before distributing the flow to your users. Make sure to test with different personas.

Chapter 9, Flow Orchestration

1. Stages are a collection of steps, whereas steps are specific flows. Stages run sequentially, whereas steps can run sequentially or concurrently.

2. Orchestration tasks are assigned to users during the Flow Orchestration run. They are available on the lightning record page where the users will be able to complete their work tasks assigned to them via Flow Orchestration.

3. There are two main types of Flow Orchestration:

    *   Autolaunched Orchestration
    *   Record-Triggered Orchestration

4. Work Guide is a lighting component on your record page. Orchestrations let us personalize tasks and action items so that business users can view and complete their tasks on each record page. When there is an interaction step in the orchestration runs, it will create a work item and assign it to a user, queue, or group as defined in the orchestration.

5. You can view all orchestration runs from the orchestration run object from App Launcher. You can see the status of your Flow Orchestration stages and steps. You also can view the orchestration run log that provides details on milestones for all your stages and steps. You can access this via **App Launcher | Orchestration Runs**.

Index

Packtpub.com

Subscribe to our online digital library for full access to over 7,000 books and videos, as well as industry leading tools to help you plan your personal development and advance your career. For more information, please visit our website.

Why subscribe?

- Spend less time learning and more time coding with practical eBooks and Videos from over 4,000 industry professionals

- Improve your learning with Skill Plans built especially for you

- Get a free eBook or video every month

- Fully searchable for easy access to vital information

- Copy and paste, print, and bookmark content

Did you know that Packt offers eBook versions of every book published, with PDF and ePub files available? You can upgrade to the eBook version at packtpub.com and as a print book customer, you are entitled to a discount on the eBook copy. Get in touch with us at customercare@packtpub.com for more details.

At www.packtpub.com, you can also read a collection of free technical articles, sign up for a range of free newsletters, and receive exclusive discounts and offers on Packt books and eBooks.

Other Books You May Enjoy

If you enjoyed this book, you may be interested in these other books by Packt:

Salesforce End-to-End Implementation Handbook

Kristian Margaryan Jørgensen

ISBN: 978-1-80461-322-1

- Discover the critical activities in Salesforce implementation
- Address common issues faced in implementing Salesforce
- Explore appropriate delivery methodology
- Understand the importance of a change management strategy
- Govern Salesforce implementation through all its phases
- Gain insights on key activities in the continuous improvement phase
- Leverage customer 360 for analytics, AI and automation

Salesforce AppExchange Success Blueprint

Jakub Stefaniak

ISBN: 978-1-83508-954-5

- Find out how to become a successful ISV partner on the AppExchange
- Understand how to tackle the challenges of AppExchange development
- Uncover how to avoid common security review pitfalls
- Discover the best practices for configuring an AppExchange listing
- Maximize the revenue potential through pricing and monetization
- Understand how to manage technical debt to maintain product quality
- Build a successful and sustainable ISV partnership with Salesforce

Packt is searching for authors like you

If you're interested in becoming an author for Packt, please visit `authors.packtpub.com` and apply today. We have worked with thousands of developers and tech professionals, just like you, to help them share their insight with the global tech community. You can make a general application, apply for a specific hot topic that we are recruiting an author for, or submit your own idea.

Share Your Thoughts

Now you've finished *Business Process Automation with Salesforce Flows*, we'd love to hear your thoughts! Scan the QR code below to go straight to the Amazon review page for this book and share your feedback or leave a review on the site that you purchased it from.

https://packt.link/r/1835089259

Your review is important to us and the tech community and will help us make sure we're delivering excellent quality content.

Download a free PDF copy of this book

Thanks for purchasing this book!

Do you like to read on the go but are unable to carry your print books everywhere?
Is your eBook purchase not compatible with the device of your choice?

Don't worry, now with every Packt book you get a DRM-free PDF version of that book at no cost.

Read anywhere, any place, on any device. Search, copy, and paste code from your favorite technical books directly into your application.

The perks don't stop there, you can get exclusive access to discounts, newsletters, and great free content in your inbox daily

Follow these simple steps to get the benefits:

1. Scan the QR code or visit the link below

https://packt.link/free-ebook/9781835089255

2. Submit your proof of purchase
3. That's it! We'll send your free PDF and other benefits to your email directly

www.ingramcontent.com/pod-product-compliance
Lightning Source LLC
Chambersburg PA
CBHW080529060326
40690CB00022B/5079